B. P. Shillaber

RHYMES

WITH REASON AND WITHOUT.

BY

B. P. SHILLABER.

Do I not represent myself to the life? Enough; all the world knows me in my book, and my book in me. — MONTAIGNE.

BOSTON:
ABEL TOMPKINS AND B. B. MUSSEY & CO.
1853.

Stereotyped by
HOBART & ROBBINS,
BOSTON.

TO

Col. Charles G. Greene,

THROUGH WHOSE INDULGENCE THE WRITER
WAS FIRST INDUCED TO EMBARK
ON THE TIDE OF RHYME,

THIS BOOK

IS RESPECTFULLY INSCRIBED.

PREFACE.

The author of the following is too old an offender to expect to be shielded from criticism by any pretence of verdancy, and he puts in no claim for critical clemency on that account; but he would ask consideration for the fact that all he has written was merely intended, originally, to amuse the writer himself, and such newspaper readers as might venture upon its perusal in the corner of their favorite journal. He disclaims all previous intention of throwing his productions into their present form, — perhaps it would have been better had he never consented to do so, — but the importunity of many friends overcame the scruples existing in his mind, and he has herein perilled his own peace for their gratification.

Many of the articles have received a goodly share of popular commendation, for some reason; and the writer trusts the merit they possess — if any — may prove a palliative for such demerits as may be found in the rest, — too easily discoverable, he greatly fears.

The portrait accompanying is a freak of the inordinate vanity that has grown up recently in the man, in view of the lavish newspaper praise he has received, which has served to bring him out of the shadow of his own hugeness, into the broad sunlight of notoriety. A desire has been frequently expressed, by distant friends, to see the "liniments" of Mrs. Partington, and he is most happy to gratify their wish.

The writer trusts that in no instance in his book has he uttered a word or sentiment that need disturb the equanimity of the most fastidious; and though the "Rhymes without Reason" may predominate, still, as the amusement of the people was their aim, their good-nature may atone for lack of literary merit. One word he can say, however, for his entire book, — as the man said about his baby, — "It is not a very handsome baby, but it 's mine." The different phases of feeling expressed therein, whether of the mirthful or the sad, — and there is much of sadness in it, — are correct transcripts of the writer's own feelings, moved at times by grief as deep as the human heart can know, and by joys of a corresponding strength.

He leaves his book with the public, fully conscious of its imperfections, but with a latent hope that it may conduce to the pleasure of those who read it; with the hope, too, that the friendly feeling which has prompted its premature praise may not be wholly disappointed in view of its deficiencies.

CONTENTS.

THE VOICE OF THE PRESS.

How some men glory in the trophies olden,
Won from the hiding dust of grim decay,
Prizing each time-worn trifle more than golden,
That long in cobweb gloom hath lain away!—

Searching in garrets and in dark haunts dismal,
Where the lone spider holds exclusive reign;
Plunging in cellars, 'mid their depths abysmal,
Relics of eld in triumph to obtain!

Thus went a seeker on a day exploring,
Curiously peeping in each musty paper;
Behind old wainscots, and 'neath ancient flooring,
Each nook illuming with a sickly taper.

Suddenly, standing on an elevation,
Peering high up on shelves above his head,
He heard a voice that to his trepidation
Said, in plain English, "Just get off my bed!"

Closer he peered into the nook before him,
And marvelled much such utterance to hear;
Sounded the ceiling all around and o'er him,
With curiosity allied with fear!

When, through the struggle of his yearning vision,
The darkness yielded to its earnestness,
Dimly appeared none other apparition
Than the worn relics of an ancient Press.

Grimly it rested in its corner dusty,
Where in forgetfulness obscure it lay;
Worm-eaten, old, and rickety, and rusty,
Memorial sad of days long passed away.

Gazing upon it with a wonder glowing,
Fancy endowed the ancient frame with tongue;
And, as he gazed, like music olden flowing,
This song it to the listener said or sung.

THE SONG OF THE PRESS.

Crazy and old, crazy and old,
I 'm left to a drear decay;
My destiny 's done, my story is told;
Yet, though oblivion's clouds enfold,
By one reflection I 'm still consoled,
I have *worn* myself away;
And though with rubbish I 'm now enrolled,
I have lived to bless my day.

Dark times were they when to birth I sprang,
Ready armed for the fight;
When trumpet-like my loud voice rang,
Awaking the nations with its clang,

Or my joyful notes of triumph sang,
  As Error took its flight, —
Wounded, fled, with many a pang,
  In Truth's enkindled light.

For the people, the people, I 've ever spoke,
  To their call I 've ever sprang;
Never in vain did they aid invoke;
My voice the sleeping Samsons woke,
And urged the speedy avenging stroke;
  In thunder tones it rang,
When Cromwell rived the tyrant's yoke,
  And heavenly Milton sang.

In later days its tones were heard
  On our own beloved shore,
And quick in the minds of men it stirred,
As greedy ears drank in its word,
Prompting deeds which no fears deterred,
  Or gloomy doubts cast o'er;
Waking hopes not to be deferred,
  To be put to rest no more.

Alas! and thus I am thrust away
  To an ignominious lot;
Mouldering, mouldering day by day,
No sunbeam visits my bed with its ray,
No laurel wreaths round my head now play,
  And, chained to this dismal spot,
The friend of Franklin and Faust now may,
  E'en like them, die and rot.

The old press thus its dismal ditty ended,
And with emotion creaked in every joint;
No strain of hope was with its sorrow blended,—
Backward, all backward, did it look and point.

"My dear old friend," thus then did speak the mortal,
"Still from the past your consolation borrow;
Don't look a moment through the future's portal,
But find in what you 've done 'surcease from sorrow.'

"You cannot be surprised to be unheeded,
When you contrast your feebleness of power
With younger presses, now that, lightning speeded,
Ten tokens give us for your one an hour.

"So lie right down and talk yourself to sleep,
Like some old crones we have out 'neath the sun,
Who, with an everlasting dulness, keep
Vexing our ears with tales of what they 've done."

THE POOR MAN'S WEALTH.

I BOAST no broad ancestral lands,
   No towers of lofty pride;
I have no niche where Mammon stands,
   For worship deified;
Mine is no lofty sounding name,
   Allied with deeds of note,
To draw the meed of loud acclaim
   From many a brawling throat.

What is the wealth that crowns the great,
   To treasures of the soul!
Let me enjoy my poor estate,
   Beyond the world's control,
The rich man's lot I 'll envy not,
   His life of downy ease;
They are not worth a passing thought,
   Compared with scenes like these.

There 's music in the gentle stream
   That murmurs near my door;
There 's beauty in the sun's bright beam
   That gilds the meadow o'er.

The insect sings upon the flower,
  The bird upon the tree;
All mine — all mine — great Nature's dower —
  They shine and sing *for me!*

See yon lake, flashing in the light,
  O'er which the white sails glide!
Show me a scene more bravely bright,
  Or one of richer pride:
I care not who the lake may own, —
  If great or rich he be, —
Its market-worth is *his* alone,
  Its beauty is for *me!*

See yonder hill its head uprear,
  And frown upon the plain!
I bless the grandeur pictured there,
  To endlessly remain;
The mountain breeze I love to feel —
  This lesson it instils:
The town enslaves with bonds of steel,
  There 's freedom on the hills.

The rich, upon their beds of down,
  Know not the joy I claim
When sunbeams first yon summit crown
  With dyes of heavenly flame;
My soul soars upwards with the lay
  That Nature's myriads raise,
And greets the newly wakened day
  With thankfulness and praise.

Give me my cottage by the hill,
  My life of humble fare,
My little plot of earth to till,
  And love my home to share,
A heart to feel for others' pain, —
  Content with this, and health,
My lips should never once complain,
  Nor ask for more of wealth.

YOUNG GRIMES.

Old Grimes is dead, that good old man,
We ne'er shall see *him* more;
But he has left a son, who bears
The name that old Grimes bore.

He wears a coat of latest cut,
His hat is new and gay;
He cannot bear to view distress,
So turns from it away.

His pants are gaiters, fitting snug
O'er patent-leather shoes;
His hair is by a barber curled;
He smokes cigars, and chews.

A chain of massive gold is borne
Above his flashy vest;
His clothes are better, every day,
Than were old Grimes's best.

He wears a gold watch in his fob,
From it hang golden seals;
He daily drives around the town
Behind a horse's heels.

In fashion's courts he constant walks,
  Where he delight doth shed;
His hands are white and very soft,
  But softer is his head.

He 's six feet tall, no post more straight,
  His teeth are pearly white;
In habits he is sometimes loose,
  And sometimes very tight.

His manners are of sweetest grace,
  His voice of softest tone;
His diamond pin 's the very one
  That old Grimes used to own.

His jetty hair conceals his mouth,
  His whiskers hide his cheek;
He has an aunt of Christian mould,
  Of temper mild and meek.

A dickey tall adorns his face,
  His neck a scarf of blue;
He sometimes goes to church, for change,
  And sleeps in Grimes's pew.

He sports the fastest "crab" in town,
  Is always quick to bet;
He never knows who 's President,
  But thinks "old Tip" 's in yet.

He dissipates the cash most free,
  Is lavish as the air;
I grieve to hear, from those who know,
  That sometimes he will swear.

He has drunk wines of every kind,
  And liquors cold and hot;
Young Grimes, in short, is just that sort
  Of man *Old* Grimes was *not*.

BALLAD OF THE PISCATAQUA.

[A SLIGHT AFFECTATION OF THE ANTIQUE.]

BLOODY FIGHT POINT.*

In the younger days of the colonies,
When minions of the king held sway,
Ere the towns in pride began to rise
By swift Piscataqua,

Beside its ever-restless tide
Lay two plantations fair;
A fertile point did them divide,
Of excellence most rare.

Then out spoke Captain Wiggin, bold, —
Captain Thomas was he hight, —
"This point is goodly to behold,
With richest worth bedight;

* A severe contest arose between the agents of the two plantations (now Dover and Portsmouth) respecting the settlement of a point of land which extended into the river from the south-western shore, and which was equally convenient for both plantations. Wiggin began to make improvements upon it; Neal ordered him to desist. Wiggin persisted, and threatened to defend his right by the sword; Neal replied in the same determined manner, and they would have proceeded to extremities, if some more moderate persons had not persuaded them to refer the dispute to their employers. From these circumstances the contested place was called "Bloody Fight Point," and still retains that name. — *Adams' Annals of Portsmouth.*

"And here I 'll plant the yellow grain,
And here the axe shall sound,
And golden crops shall crowd my wain,
And plenty aye abound."

Then up spake Captain Walter Neal —
"Now, by my faith, not so!
To weapons dire I 'll make appeal,
Ere onward thus thou 'lt go.

"For unto the Lower Plantation
Doth this fair point belong,
And I, for its full possession,
Will battle long and strong."

Then stoutly spoke Captain Thomas,
For a gallant man was he:
"When you 're able to take it from us,
To yield it I 'll agree."

Then Captain Neal turned deadly white,
Brim full was he of rage;
He ground his teeth in fearful spite,
And threatened war to wage.

And Captain Thomas Wiggin, he
Looked stern and very wroth,
And vowed a fight he 'd like to see,
For combat nothing loth.

Great woe did seize good people then,
  Such sad thing for to see,
As two so gallant gentlemen
  Thus sorely disagree.

And interposéd did their word,
  The discord to allay;
And peace again their bosoms stirred,
  Before so fierce for fray.

Then "Bloody Fight Point" that spot was hight;
  Not from its hue, I ween,
Nor yet for its ensanguined fight,
  But for blood it *might* have seen,

Had Captain Wiggin and Captain Neal
  There met in mortal fight,
And the arbitration of biting steel
  Had settled their quarrel right.

Now Bloody Fight Point is a peaceful spot,
  On Newington's tranquil shore,
And Neal and Wiggin are both forgot,
  Save in history's musty lore.

THE EARTH AND THINGS.

Some people love to groan over the text that "the earth is waxing old, like a garment."

THE brave old earth in space is swinging
  As gayly as when God first arrayed her,
When the stars of morn with joy were singing
  Praises to Him whose hand had made her;
Her bowers as green, and her flowers as bright
  As brightly shining the sun around her,
As when its newly-kindled light
  In the darksome gloom of chaos found her.

What to her is the paltry year,
  That makes the calendar of the mortal?
In the onward march of her career,
  She has but entered at its portal;
Rejoicing yet in her pride and bloom,
  She rolleth around her track diurnal,
No nearer seeming her day of doom
  Than when first formed by the great Eternal.

The heaving deep makes loud acclaim
  To heaven, which answereth back the chorus,
While earthquake tones, 'mid smoke and flame,
  Join in the peal with note sonorous;

The hurricano's boisterous breath
  Wildly soundeth o'er land and ocean,
Bearing here to a quick-sped death,
  And there awaking to stern commotion.

The birds sing sweet in the leafy trees,
  The bees are humming in summer bowers,
And the blandly-blowing western breeze
  Is wafting wide the odor of flowers;
The water-rills are speeding along,
  And is heard the fountain's music rushing,
And the human heart beats time to the song
  That on every side is in melody gushing.

All go to form the anthem grand,
  From the earthquake's sound to the rippling river,
Harmonious singing o'er sea and land,
  As at beginning, so on forever!
As grandly now is the anthem ringing,
  In earth, as when God first arrayed her;
When the stars of morn with joy were singing
  Praises to Him whose hand had made her.

LITTLE EMMA GOING TO SLEEP.

Sweet night-capped traveller to the realm of dreams,
  Now droops thine eye towards its calm repose;
Forgotten are the various joyous schemes
  And childish fancies that before thee rose.

The day was all too short for their employ,
  And the fast waning of the autumn sun
Curbed the swift current of thy noisy joy,
  That bore thee onward till the day was done.

The last beam fadeth from thy gentle eye,
  Sleep claims dominion, and beneath its sway
Thy spirit on unfettered wing may fly
  From earth and its allurements far away;

To drink, perchance, from some celestial rill,
  To breathe a purer atmosphere than ours,
To hear blest notes from angel harps distil.
  To catch sweet odors from immortal flowers;

To view fair scenes bright spirits lead thee through,
  Clothed in the beauteous hues that Faith reveals,
Until the day again its sway renew,
  And its first dawning thy bright eye unseals.

O, could we sink thus calmly to our rest,
  Who, older grown, have felt the weight of care!
We seek our pillows with a troubled breast,
  And weary hours of thought attend us there.

My child! I bend me gently o'er thy bed,
  And listen to thy breathing soft and light;
A soothing influence doth its calmness shed,
  And innocence here sanctifies the night.

THE POOR FARM.

THE traveller man looketh over the wall
  Where the pauper poor is hoeing;
The corn is sickly and very small,
  As if too weak to be growing.

And the leaves on the trees are sparse and dry,
  And the weeds are so thin and drooping,
They scarcely the strength of the pauper try,
  As he for their ruin is stooping.

"Old fellow," then cried the traveller man,
  As he looked there over the wall,
"Is n't this the spot, — just say, if you can, —
  That people the 'Poor Farm' call?"

Then the pauper rested upon his hoe,
  And the traveller man he scanned,
As he wiped his hand on his trousers of tow,
  And then wiped his brow with his hand.

"The 'poor farm,' I fegs!" quoth the pauper poor,
  "And well may they call it so;
For, 'tween you and me and the work-house door,
  'T is the *poorest* farm I know."

Then loudly did laugh the pauper bold, —
He laughed with a goodly cheer,
And the traveller's blood ran chill and cold
Such levity to hear.

'Tis bad in the reckless city's round
To list to the horrid pun,
But it comes with a force far more profound
From the lips of a work-house one.

POVERTY IN A SHOWER.

"The rough river ran." — HOOD.

ONE more unfortunate,
  Wet to the skin,
Very importunate,
  Wants to get in.

Take him up speedily,
  Stop now the 'bus;
What care though seedily
  Looks he to us?

See, the poor fellow
Has got no umbrella,
  Whilst the rain patters,
Soaking his jacket,
  Hanging in tatters! —
Tin, doth he lack it?

Treat him not scornfully,
He is not corned fully,
  He is thy brother;
Open thy door for him,
Show him there 's store for him —
  Room for another.

Make no deep studying
Into his muddying,
   Damp and unhealthy;
Rain is a leveller, —
Treat the poor traveller
   Well as if wealthy.

Alas for the rarity
Of practical charity
   Under the sun!
O! it is pitiful,
In a whole city full,
   'Brel has he none.

Stands on the sidewalk,
After a wide walk,
   Money all spent;
His deep pocket feeling,
No cash there revealing,
   Not a red cent!

The cold April storms
   Make him tremble like aspen;
No 'bus opes its arms,
   His form to be clasping;
Mad at the luck of it,
Sad at the duck of it,
   Glad to be ta'en
Anywhere, anywhere
   Out of the rain.

Take him up speedily,
  Man of the 'bus;
Poor, he looks seedily,
  Poorer his purse.

In he steps gloomily,
Don't think contumely,
Don't make a pother, —
He is thy brother,
  Sad and distrest;
Be *now* his protector,
Then leave the collector
  To settle the rest!

THE SKELETON SCHOONER.

THE moon comes up from Dorchester,
   From Dorchester behind,
And gloomy clouds scud through the sky,
   Borne on the midnight wind;

And stillness broods above the land,
   A stillness strange and dread,
Like the hush of terror-stricken men
   In presence of the dead.

Upon South Boston's upper bridge
   I take my pensive stand,
And gaze upon the rippling waves,
   And on the shadowy land.

I gaze upon the watery waves
   That wander there away,
Where the skeleton dark of the shattered bark
   Is shown in the moon's dim ray.

I see her low in her loneliness
   Lean on her leaky side;
Her masts are bowed, and, void of shroud,
   Hang listless o'er the tide;

And here and there upon the air
  The ropes swing wildly free,
As if they 'd fain to feel again
  The heaving of the sea.

And high up on the drooping masts
  The rotting halyards scream,
And the sounds take form in my fancy warm
  Of voices in a dream.

She rights! she rights! — afloat once more —
  I see her peopled deck,
And her white sails gleam in the pale moonbeam
  Withouten shade or speck.

Now on and on, in the teeth of the wind,
  That ghostly vessel glides;
No ripple, I trow, from her rushing prow,
  No gleam from her moss-grown sides.

And her sails hang idly swinging,
  As if God's blessed gale
Withheld its aid, or was afraid
  To fill that spectral sail.

Still on and on, o'er the waters blue,
  Nor heeding wind nor tide,
Like phantom dread from realms of the dead,
  The skeleton bark doth glide.

A light! — a blue and ghastly glare —
  Shoots upward from below,
And the shadowy men and the shadowy ship
  Are shown in its hideous glow.

A frightful shriek disturbs the air! —
  A shriek both loud and clear,
That echoes around to the distant bound,
  Which my spirit shrinks to hear.

My doom be stayed! — 't was thus I prayed,
  As a demon shook my arm.
"Say," cried a voice, "don't be afraid,
  I don't mean ye any harm!"

'T was the watch — and there on the bridge I 'd slept,
  In the midnight damp and chill;
And the skeleton gray before me lay
  All dreary, and dark, and still.

THE SUMMER RAIN.

THE farmer's heart was sad, his toil was vain,
His famished crops were crisping in the field,
For not one drop of life-sustaining rain
Did the red clouds of summer deign to yield.

The cattle 'neath the trees, with lolling tongue,
Gave up the search for herbage in despair,
And listless in the shade their heads they hung,
And chewed their cuds with most desponding air.

The brook was dry, or stood, a muddy pool,
Whose stagnant waters none might dare to drink,
Which late, in crystal brightness, pure and cool,
Wooed with its song the thirsty to its brink.

The burning sun drank up the pearly dew
That evening, pitying, on creation shed,
And o'er the parchéd earth his hot beams threw—
The herbage sickened and the flowers lay dead.

The river shimmered in his lurid rays,
The corn grew dry and withered as it stood,
The fainting birds scarce raised their tuneful lays
In dim recesses of the ancient wood.

Then man and vegetation prayed for rain —
  The withered stalks, like famished hands, were raised;
But day by day was man's petition vain,
  The clouds arose and vanished as he gazed.

At length the blessed boon, so long withheld,
  Came like an angel down in man's dismay,
Cheering the heart that well-nigh had rebelled,
  And giving joy where grief erewhile held sway.

The thirsty earth drank in, with greedy tongue,
  The cooling flood that trickled o'er its breast;
The trees abroad their arms enraptured flung,
  And grass and flower once more upreared their crest;

The brooks again resumed their gladsome song,
  And through the meadows took their cheerful way;
Once more the corn its verdant pennons flung,
  Once more the birds made merry on the spray.

The farmer's heart grew glad, and on his knee,
  His voice attuned with warm devotion's strain,
He poured his soul in gratitude to see
  The blessed coming of the summer rain —

Which falls, like God's own spirit, on the dust
  Of man's fallen nature, dead in sin and pain,
Till with a newer hope and holier trust
  It wakens into life and joy again.

UNFAILING SIGNS.

WHEN the wind blows from the orient
  Be certain it will rain;
When the wind blows from the occident
  'T will soon be fair again.

Good Mrs. Goodwin hung her line,
  And called for her maiden Ann;
For the day was fair and the day was fine,
  And she her washing began.

And her face was bright
  With joy and hope,
And her clothes were white
  With soda and soap,
And over the tub she wrung and wrung,
While merrily, merrily ran her tongue,
As on to the line her clothes she flung;
  And out on the air,
  Like banners fair,
The garments fluttered with freedom rare.

But the wind blew east, and her neighbor said
  That it boded rain and trouble,
And the water that simmered on the crane
  Rose up in many a bubble.

But good Mrs. Goodwin kept right on,
  Nor heeded the tokens plain;
She should have known, the foolish one!
  That it boded naught but rain;

She should have seen that the wind was east,
  And spared her present toil,—
'T is a hard, hard thing those clothes to wring,
  And harder to have them spoil.

Good Mrs. Goodwin heard never a word,
  But kept on with her wringing,
And though the wind blew most dismally blue,
  She lightened her care with singing.

But her neighbor knew,
And all day through
  She watched for rain and squall;
But the sun shone bright,
In her despite,
  And it did n't rain at all.

Then good Mrs. Goodwin laughed right loud,
  O, merrily laughéd she!—
Who watch for rain may watch in vain;
  Best wait till it comes, like me.

'T is best not borrow the woe of to-morrow
  To-day's enjoyment to crowd,
If the sun shines bright, improve its light,
  Nor think of to-morrow's cloud.

WHAT WAS IT ALL ABOUT?

WRITTEN IN REFERENCE TO THE GREAT RAILROAD JUBILEE OF 1851.

The City of Boston " gin a treat,"
  And folks came far and near to see,
And all who had the good luck to see 't
  In praise thereof did loudly agree,
And said that for splendor it could n't be beat,
  'Cause everything was given 'em free.

President and Governors all were there,
  And Elgin's lord, and the Lord knows who,
And mighty men from everywhere,
  With some that were n't so mighty, too;
And ladies rich and ladies fair
  Looked smilingly on, as they always do.

And steamers, with streamers all afloat,
  Gallantly ploughed Massachusetts Bay,
That strangers might have a chance to note,
  By a look at the water, just how the land lay;
But the salt in the air parched every throat, —
  That water would n't relieve, they say.

But on board there luckily chanced to be
  Whole baskets full of the "Newark brand,"
And, though obnoxious to those like me,
  The corks popped briskly on every hand;

It was a most spirited sight to see,
That the shoreman rarely views on land.

The streets with bunting were gayly spread,
They colors of every kind did don;
It needed a head extensively read
All their significance to con;
But some sagaciously winked, and said
That Boston was putting her flannels on.

And the people made a stir in the fun,
And had "the Trades" all a-marching out,
With banners and mottoes, every one,
And workmen a-working, with muscles stout;
Though we question if many a mother's son
Could tell what the hubbub was all about.

And marshals and aids, upon coursers gay,
"And constables with painted poles,"
And soldiers, ready for warlike fray,
All candidates for immortal scrolls,
Swelled up the pageant which graced the day,
But what 't was for did n't vex their souls.

Men met to feast, and the speakers spoke;
O, long and loud did the spouters spout!
And many a jibe and many a joke
Did the "grand occasion" worry out;
There was much of fire, but more of smoke,
But few knew what it was all about.

Well, the City of Boston "gin a treat,"
  And the people relished the noise and rout,
Their voices were heard in every street,
  Hurraing loudly with lungs most stout;
But we guess, of all who were there to see 't,
  Very few knew what 't was all about.

MYSTERIOUS RAPPINGS.

LATE one evening I was sitting, gloomy shadows round me flitting, —
Mrs. Partington, a-knitting, occupied the grate before;
Suddenly I heard a patter, a slight and very trifling matter,
As if it were a thieving rat or mouse within my closet door;
A thieving and mischievous rat or mouse within my closet door, —
Only this, and nothing more.

Then all my dreaminess forsook me; rising up, I straightway shook me,
A light from off the table took, and swift the rat's destruction swore;
Mrs. P. smiled approbation on my prompt determination,
And without more hesitation oped I wide the closet door;
Boldly, without hesitation opened wide the closet door;
Darkness there, and nothing more!

As upon the sound I pondered, what the deuce it was I wondered;
Could it be my ear had blundered, as at times it had before?

But scarce again was I reseated, ere I heard the sound repeated,
The same dull patter that had greeted me from out the closet door;
The same dull patter that had greeted me from out the closet door;
A gentle patter, nothing more.

Then my rage arose unbounded, — "What," cried I, "is this confounded
Noise with which my ear is wounded — noise I 've never heard before?
If 't is presage dread of evil, if 't is made by ghost or devil,
I call on ye to be more civil — 'stop that knocking at the door!'
Stop that strange mysterious knocking there, within my closet door;
Grant me this, if nothing more."

Once again I seized the candle, rudely grasped the latchet's handle,
Savage as a Goth or Vandal, that kicked up rumpuses of yore, —
"What the dickens is the matter," said I, "to produce this patter?"
To Mrs. P., and looked straight at her. "I don't know," said she, "I 'm shore;
Lest it be a pesky rat, or something, I don't know, I 'm shore."
This she said, and nothing more.

Still the noise kept on unceasing; evidently 'twas increasing;
Like a cart-wheel wanting greasing, wore it on my nerves full sore;
Patter, patter, patter, patter, the rain the while made noisy clatter,
My teeth with boding ill did chatter, as when I 'm troubled by a bore—
Some prosing, dull, and dismal fellow, coming in but just to bore;
Only this, and nothing more.

All night long it kept on tapping; vain I laid myself for napping,
Calling sleep my sense to wrap in darkness till the night was o'er;
A dismal candle, dimly burning, watched me as I lay there turning,
In desperation wildly yearning that sleep would visit me once more;
Sleep, refreshing sleep, did I most urgently implore;
This I wished, and nothing more.

With the day I rose next morning, and, all idle terror scorning,
Went to finding out the warning that annoyed me so before;
When straightway, to my consternation, daylight made the revelation
Of a scene of devastation that annoyed me very sore,
Such a scene of devastation as annoyed me very sore;
This it was, and nothing more:

The rotten roof had taken leaking, and the rain, a passage seeking,
Through the murky darkness sneaking, found my hat-box on the floor;
There, exposed to dire disaster, lay my bran-new Sunday castor,
And its hapless, luckless master ne'er shall see its beauties more —
Ne'er shall see its glossy beauty, that his glory was before;
It is gone, forevermore!

THE CONSUMPTIVE.

SHE faded, O, she faded !
  And the roses fled her cheek,
And her voice, that carolled like a bird's,
  Grew tremulous and weak !
Her parched lips softly whispered
  The sweet words she would say,
And her cold, thin hand was pale and still
  As the sheet whereon it lay.

But her spirit glowed the brighter,
  As her mortal end drew nigh, —
It beamed with heavenly radiance
  In the lustre of her eye ;
She seemed to borrow glories
  From the world she nearer drew,
And, as the form of earth decayed,
  Her angel nature grew.

And patiently, how patiently!
  She pressed her bed of pain,
As, sun by sun, the days declined,
  And then renewed again ;
Her Father's hand she recognized,
  And kissed the chastening rod,
And calmly waited for the hour
  When she should soar to God.

And friends who gathered round her
  Took comfort from her tone;
They felt that she was not for earth's,
  But heaven's joys alone;
And when the angel severed
  The ties that bound her here,
Her transit filled their hearts with joy—
  Their own loss claimed a tear.

O, Death! when thus approaching,
  An angel form you take,
And pour the healing balm for hearts
  That otherwise might break,
We see thy path a way of light,
  Ascending to the sky,
And pray an end thus fraught with bliss—
  A death thus blest to die.

THE SONG OF THE JILTED ONE.

A sweeter girl I never knew
  Than Juliana Lownds, —
A lump of loveliness she grew,
  And weighed two hundred pounds.

Her form majestic was and straight,
  It queenly graces bore,
And as she walked she showed a gait
  Which men liked to adore.

Her voice! — ah! in it dwelt a charm, —
  One likewise in her fist;
For power great was in her arm,
  That few might dare resist.

Her skin was fair, — ah! very fair, —
  Her teeth were white as pearls;
A charming auburn was her hair,
  Which hung in corkscrew curls.

Her mouth was just that comely sort
  'T would sore provoke to kiss it, —
'T would buss you for the asking for 't,
  And never seem to miss it.

Her eyes were of the heavenly hue,
  And roguish in their beaming;
A glance would pierce the toughest through,
  And set the tender dreaming.

Her blush was like the clover red;
  Her smile, the sunbeam gay;
Her frown, the black cloud overhead;
  Her breath, the new-mown hay.

Her nose was Nature's fairest show, —
  Sculptor ne'er dreamed a richer;
Though envious ones compared it to
  The nose upon a pitcher.

And how I loved fair Julian.!
  And how I spent my money!
My life's young current seeming ran
  With naught but wine and honey.

And every hour of every day,
  With glances warm as tinder,
I watched my charmer o'er the way,
  As she worked by a "winder."

Alas! how human hopes decay!
  How love's repasts grow colder!
We dine on strawberries to-day,
  To-morrow get cold shoulder.

False Juliana cast me by,
And wedded with a baker;
We had a fight—I blacked his eye,
And let the loafer take her.

Time, time has flown, and I 'm unwed,
And Fame has been the jewel
That I with hope have worshippéd,
Nor found her cold or cruel.

And Juliana, fair no more,
Has portlier grown than ever;
A baker's dozen round her door,
A husband far from clever.

I see him reel from dram-shops low,
Most desperately wilted,
And ask myself, "Can it be so,
That I for *him* was jilted?"

And Juliana sees me pass,
I know, with thought regretful;
I hear her scold, alas! alas!
With accents harsh and fretful.

And at such times, I greatly fear,
Her seedy spouse, the baker,
May, as he quails her notes to hear,
Wish that the —— might take her.

THE OLD PRINTER.

A FANCY SKETCH, BUT TOO NEAR THE TRUTH TO MAKE MUCH FUN OF.

I SEE him at his case,
With his anxious, cheerless face,
Worn and brown;
And the types' unceasing click,
As they drop within his stick,
Seems of Life's old clock the tick,
Running down.

I 've known him many a year,
That old Type, bent and queer, —
Boy and man; —
Time was when step elate
Distinguishéd his gait,
And his form was tall and straight,
We now scan.

I 've marked him, day by day,
As he passed along the way
To his toil;
He 's labored might and main,
A living scant to gain,
And some interest small attain
In the soil.

And hope was high at first,
And the golden cheat he nursed,
 Till he found
That hope was but a glare
In a cold and frosty air,
And the promise, pictured fair,
 Barren ground.

He ne'er was reckoned bad,
But I 've seen him smile right glad
 At "*leaded*" woes,
While a dark and lowering frown
Would spread his features round,
Where virtue's praise did sound,
 If 't were "*close*."

Long years he 's labored on,
And the rosy hues are gone
 From his sky;
For others are his hours,
For others are his powers, —
His days, uncheered by flowers,
 Flitting by.

You may see him, night by night,
By the lamp's dull, dreamy light,
 Standing there;
With cobweb curtains spread
In festoons o'er his head,
That sooty showers shed
 In his hair.

And when the waning moon
Proclaims of night the noon,
    If you roam,
You may see him, weak and frail,
As his weary steps do fail,
In motion like the snail,
    Wending home.

His form by years is bent,
To his hair a tinge is lent
    Sadly gray;
And his teeth have long decayed,
And his eyes their trust betrayed, —
Great havoc Time has made
    With his clay!

But soon will come the day
When his form will pass away
    From our view,
And the spot shall know no more
The sorrows that he bore,
Or the disappointments sore
    That he knew.

THE THREE LOCKS.

I LAY them gently on my open palm —
  Three locks of hair — the golden, dark and white;
My spirit wakes from apathetic calm,
  As the known tokens greet my eager sight.

And Memory beckons from the distant past
  A train of spectral fancies to my ken;
Age, Youth and Childhood, — O, how sweet and fast
  Come love and joy to my cold heart again!

FATHER! I see thee now, as when thy prime
  Gave vigorous promise of thy lengthened years, —
That a broad lapse would intervene in time,
  Dividing present joy from future tears.

And the assurance given *was* fulfilled;
  A garner full of years was life to thee,
And when that kindly heart in death was stilled,
  We kissed the rod, and bowed to Heaven's decree.

Calmly to death, to sleep serene, thou passed;
  World-worn and weary, thou wert ready now!
Strange that my tears should flow so free and fast
  As when this lock I took from off thy brow.

BROTHER! the raven's sable plume ne'er shone
With glossier lustre in the eye of day
Than this last trophy which affection won
From the loved form that cold before me lay.

O, Death! how bitter was the pang when riven
Became the tender bond which bound him here!
O, Death! a sadder blow thou ne'er hast given
Than that which brought him to his early bier.

In the young spring-time of his days he passed
From youth's allurements and from scenes of earth,—
As the bright morning may be overcast
Ere many hours shall smile upon its birth.

MY CHILD! my dimming eyes behold thee still,
As when thy little hand in mine was pressed;
As when my pulse with rapture wild would thrill,
To feel thy young heart throb against my breast;

As when that golden curl would sweetly blend
With the bright glory of thy radiant eye,
And such a beauty to thy face did lend
As stilled the thought that thou couldst ever die;

As when thy prattling tongue would greet mine ear
With the glad accent of a dawning love;
As when thy promise made my pathway here
A blessed forecast of the bliss above.

I weave a braid, — the gold, the dark, the white, —
  They mingle well, these types of human life!
The calm of Age, Youth's hope, the Child's delight, —
  The simple cord with eloquence is rife.

Brief is the time dividing old and young —
  A step between the cradle and the grave;
Death's shadow o'er the manly oak is flung,
  Ere yet its youthful glories cease to wave.

THE MAN IN THE 'BUS.

"One pull for the right!" and he quailed as he read,
For it quickened to life a conscience long dead;
And an ocean of memories rushed through his mind
Of duties neglected, occasions declined,
Where, acting with heart and generous might,
He oft could have given "one pull for the right;" —
Occasions long past, to be recalled never,
Evanished and gone, like his power, forever!
And he mused on the text, and felt, as he mused,
Like one who was judged for past powers abused,
And he sighed that the world should have shut from the
light
That cardinal duty, to "pull for the right."
And wrong unadjusted rose up in his view, —
Old evils, world old, that had led on to new,
Where might, unregarding the right or the just,
Crushed the humble and lowly with wrongs to the dust;
Where the money-god's altar had risen on high,
And gold made the standard to gauge virtue by;
Where judges and laws against justice rebel,
And truth lies asleep in a fathomless well! —
But just as he vowed that, happen what might,
He would henceforth and evermore "pull for the right,"
"Two pulls for the left" brought him close to his door;
'T was an omnibus dream — only this — nothing more.

THE OMEN MOON.

O, I'VE seen the fair new moon, mother!
Her crescent crowns the night,
And from its silver horns, mother,
Streams forth a gentle light;
O, fair its beam,
On wood and stream,
Putting all gloom to flight;
And I saw her over my right, mother,
I saw her over my right.

On the bridge by the maple path, mother,
I stood and looked below,
And the rippling waves in the light, mother,
Shone bright with its silvery glow;
The song of a bird
The calm air stirred
Of the tranquil summer night;
And the moon shone over my right, mother,
And the moon shone over my right.

And I thought of the land of the blest, mother,
Where the holy spirits dwell,
And their smiles seemed wove with the light, mother,
Of the moonbeams, where they fell,

And my spirit turned
Where the fair stars burned
With a new and supreme delight,
As the moon shone over my right, mother,
As the moon shone over my right.

And then I wished my wish, mother,
Beneath the moon's fair beams;
Strange, strange that thoughts of earth, mother,
Should mix with our heavenly dreams!
I 'm not to blame,
I could but name
My love in my prayer to-night,
When the moon shone over my right, mother,
When the moon shone over my right.

I heard a sigh by my side, mother,
As I gazed on the wave below,
And my heart beat strangely fast, mother,
But not with fear, — O, no!
I forgot to say
John came that way,
By chance, though, doubtless, quite,
And the moon shone over *our* right, mother,
And the moon shone over our right.

THE LAUGHING BAN.

O, LAUGHTER is sweet from the lips of youth,
When it gushes forth loud and clear, —
So fraught with melody and truth,
So full of the heart's own cheer!

And rich is the laugh of the jocund one,
Whom a happy soul pervades;
'T is nature's voice, as when streams rejoice
Through the flowery summer glades.

For the heart is a stream, on whose crystal tide
Its feelings and passions throng;
Some darkling and low in mystery glide,
Some laughingly move along.

O, could you have seen fair Annabel Green,
With her eyes so bright and blue,
And her hair of gold that gleaming rolled
O'er her neck of Parian hue!

Her laugh was as gay as the song of birds
In the leafy bowers of spring,
And her breath was sweet as the odors that meet
Where the gales their fragrance fling.

O, why did she laugh at the weirdly wife,
At the tale of her grievous woe?
The stamp of her crime, in death and in life,
Will mark her steps below.

'T was a terrible sin, and the red curse fell
Like a blight upon her heart!
It haunted her sleep with a sorrow deep,
And with day would not depart.

Laugh! ay, laugh when the morning sun
Unbars the gates of day,
And laugh when the streams of its golden beams
In the bright west fade away;

And laugh when the gloom of midnight sits
Like a nightmare on your breast,
And laugh when the shadow of sorrow flits
O'er your soul in its sad unrest;

And laugh at another's pain and strife,
And the misery that distils
From the leaves of the Upas of human life,
And its branches of deadly ills!

The years flew by, and, asleep or awake,
Was her ill-timed laughter heard,
When her heart with the tremor of fear did shake,
And when with grief 't was stirred.

And she died with a laugh upon her lips,
  That laugh so wild and shrill,
And her eyes were closed in the drear eclipse,
  But the laugh remained there still.

This moral clearly my tale imparts: —
  You may laugh in your innocent glee,
But banish scorn from your blithesome hearts,
  Nor mock at misery;
Lest the fate we have seen of Annabel Green
  May likewise hap to thee.

THE JOUR. PRINTER'S MONUMENT.

A MYSTERY.

Poor Pi, the printer, was woesome sick,
And he lay on his bed to die;
His eye was glazed, and his breath was thick,
And Death with his dart gave Pi a stick,
Life's frail bucket he over did kick,
And a senseless heap lay Pi.

'T was sad to see his form thus laid,
So ghastly and so stark;
Care on his brow deep lines had made,
And if ever the rays of joy there played,
'T was but for a moment, and then to fade,
Like meteors 'mid the dark.

His body was placed in a humble case,
And borne from his garret dim;
And sighs were heaved that in Death's embrace
Thus had determined his hard-run race;
Friends prayed for his soul as they looked on his face;
What were tears or prayers to him?

They left him to moulder beneath the sod,
And return to primal dust;
They knew he'd long felt affliction's rod,—

Small comfort was there in the path he had trod,
And they felt that while he mixed with the clod
His spirit was with the just.

Now Time passed on, — long years rolled by,
And Memory 'waked the past;
Men sought the grave of the printer Pi,
A pillar to rear, both broad and high,
As if to atone for old ill to try,
And justice do at last.

'T was no marble column that upward rose
To tower amid the clouds;
Nor granite shaft to record his woes,
Of his hopes all crushed and his heart all froze; —
These were not what the builders chose,
To draw admiring crowds.

But they dragged from its nook the ancient press
That of yore had caused him pain —
The tongue of thought which, through his distress,
Had spoken in tones the world to bless —
The dust of years on its frame did rest,
And many a time-worn stain.

They made it their chiefest corner-stone,
Then piled the mass amain;
The cross-legged bank 'neath a heap did groan,
The ink-balls and the trough were thrown,
The ink-block, cobweb over-grown,
The mallet and the plane.

And hard old cases, in grim array,
  And chases thick with rust,
And quoin-drawers long since thrown away,
And relics snatched from a doomed decay,
Were brought again to the light of day,
  All clothed in ancient dust.

Then they gathered the toil and the mental pain
  Which had marked his earthly race;
And they gathered the hours to him all vain,
Where others had reaped the accruing gain,
And the bitter thoughts which his soul did stain,
  And the sweat of his care-worn face.

A crowning piece for the pile they sought,
  And long they sought in vain;
Till a gleam of joy or two they brought,
And Saturday nights that with rest were fraught,
And moments of calm and pleasant thought,
  When "fat" he'd chanced to gain.

Then Wisdom's light was shed on the scene,
  And a goodly sight was there;
The incongruous mass had changed its mien,
And, glowing bright in celestial sheen,
Its summit resting the stars between,
  Rose the pile through the upper air.

And Earth grew glad amid the light
  Diffusive in its ray;
And darkened spots came grandly bright,

With new-found radiance bedight,—
As sunshine followeth the night,—
  And smiles upon the day.

Effulgently beamed its glories forth,
  And then from far and nigh
Came sages, as erst when Truth had birth,
The wise and mighty children of earth,
And laid their tribute of mind to worth
  On the urn of the printer Pi.

And then this riddle was plainly read:
  That he lives not in vain
Who wrestles with woe to heart and head,
Till the breath is stilled and sense is dead,
And stretches his form on a martyr's bed:
  For a darkened world shall gain.

THE WIDOW OF NODDLE'S ISLAND.

AN IMITATION.

A FOG was coming swiftly from the ocean,
Just at the close of day,
When through the window-panes, with strange emotion,
Looked the fair Widow May.

She looked out on the river and Deer Island,
And the white walls of Lynn;
Plainly she saw, from glance at sea and highland,
A storm was setting in.

Charlestown and Chelsea, Hull, Nahant and Boston,
Were all seen dim and gray,
Fading 'mid sea-clouds they would soon be lost in,
When daylight died away.

Sullen and silent, and like blankets sombre,
Those clouds throughout the night
Frightened the lonely Widow from her slumber,
And made her cheek turn white.

And now they poured at dawn their deep libations,
  On every town and hill;
Cloud answering cloud, with washy salutations,
  As mortals often will.

And down the coast, all drowning field and meadow,
  They roar for many a mile,
As if to waken from her sleep the Widow
  Of Noddle's famous Isle.

Her shall no thunder from the cloud's dark quiver,
  No rain-drops on the wall,
No morning shout from boatmen on the river,
  Awaken with their call!

Because, there watching, with an eye to leeward,
  The long line of the coast,
Stands the lone Widow gazing wildly seaward,
  Still wakeful on her post.

For in the night was one, exposed to peril,
  In sombre darkness hid,
Loved by the Widow fair, and surnamed Merrill,
  And captain of the Squid.

He sailed upon the wild, tempestuous billow,
  The dark and silent deep,
And at the thought sleep fled the Widow's pillow,
  Too sorrowful for sleep.

The wind refrained not from its wild outpouring,
  But smote the widow sore;
Ah, what a blow! that went through Boston roaring,
  And whitened all the shore.

But the next day came up a stiff nor'wester,
  The sun rose bright o'erhead;
The Squid returned, and, as the captain pressed her,
  The widow's terror fled.

THE SPRING ON THE SHORE.*

UPGUSHING through the pebbly strand,
Here flows a fairy crystal stream;
Its waters, sparkling o'er the sand,
Like threads of liquid silver seem.

The music of its note is sweet,
As singingly it speeds along,
The river's stormy lord to meet,
And soothe his harshness with a song.

The cattle from the grassy lea
Come gratefully its wealth to drink,
And birds of land and birds of sea
Meet peacefully beside its brink.

The sunbeam on the rippling tide
Smiles gayly down from heavenly height,
To see its glories magnified
In myriad beams of golden light.

And men, with foreheads red and warm,
Bow down before the crystal shrine;
And girlhood bends her graceful form,
And shadowy lips with real join.

* Upon the shore of the Piscataqua, in Newington, N. H., is a spring of pure water, over which the salt river flows at every high tide. It was suggestive of the poem.

But see the rapid river rise!
  Fast, fast it gains upon the shore, —
A moment, and the spot we prize
  The angry billow closes o'er.

But gushing still, though hid from view,
  The little rill yet pours its tide,
As constantly, as pure and true,
  As when by sunlight glorified!

And when the rolling river wanes,
  And cravenly deserts the shore,
The rivulet new strength obtains,
  And sings and sparkles as before.

And this the lesson it may teach:
  That thus Truth's crystal streamlets rise,
And trickle on o'er Time's dark beach,
  To bless the heart and glad the eyes.

And that, though Error's tide o'erflow
  The gentle stream, and hide its power,
Its silvery wave again will glow,
  And Truth's fair spirit rule the hour.

MRS. PARTINGTON AT TEA.

Good Mistress P.
Sat sipping her tea,
Sipping it, sipping it, Isaac and she;
What though the wind blew fiercely around,
And the rain on the pane gave a comfortless sound?
Little cared she,
Kind Mistress P.,
As Isaac and she sat sipping their tea.

And in memory
What sights did she see,
As Isaac and she sat sipping their tea!
She turned her gaze to the opposite wall,
Where hung the profile of Corporal Paul,
And fancies free,
To Mistress P.,
Arose in her mind like the steam of the tea.

And little saw she,
Blind Mistress P.,
As silently she sat sipping her tea,—

With her eyes on the wall and her mind away,—
That Isaac was taking the time to play:
And wicked was he
To Mistress P.,
As dreamily she sat sipping her tea.

For Isaac he,
In diablerie,
Emptied her rappee into her tea;
And the old dame tasted and tasted on,
Till she thought, good soul, that her taste was gone,
For the souchong tea
And the strong rappee
Sorely puzzled the palate of Mistress P.

MORAL.

This moral, you see,
Is drawn from the tea
That Isaac had ruined for Mistress P.:
Forever will mix in the cup of our joy
The dark rappee of sorrow's alloy,
And none are free,
Any more than she,
From annoying alloys that mix with their tea.

THE SENSITIVE MAN was at a concert one night, and in the seat directly before him was a knit jacket, of most exquisite mould, encircling a form of faultless symmetry. Above the jacket arose a charming neck, about which played, in golden dalliance, a wave of brilliant curls. His heart was a-glow at once. He saw nothing but the jacket and curls, for the face was turned away; and, taking out his pencil, he wrote a burning sonnet to the "Jacket of Blue" on the crown of his hat. The sonnet burned up by self-combustion; but the recollection of the feeling that occasioned it yet remains, and the theme of his ardent soul is now

THE JACKET OF BLUE.

'T WAS a neat little, sweet little jacket of blue,
With trimming of fur all encompassed around it,
And fastened with ribbons of loveliest hue,
Which girdled the beautiful apex that crowned it.
I gazed on the vesture like one in a dream,
My fancy took wing as I pondered upon it,
And quicker than thought the delectable theme
Had taken the form of a heavenly sonnet.

That sonnet! 't was rapture's most exquisite tone,
Poured forth from a soul by ecstasy haunted;
Alas! with its theme has the melody flown,
And fancy has wakened, but not disenchanted;
In pleasure's gay walks are my eyes still inclined
To watch for that delicate jacket's appearing,
And the beautiful neck, with ringlets entwined,
Like a lily in spring from a blue lake uprearing.

'T was a neat little, sweet little jacket of blue,
With trimming of fur all encompassed around it,
And fastened with ribbons of loveliest hue,
Which girdled the lily-white beauty that crowned it.
I owned to its thrall, and I still feel its charm, —
'T will haunt me, I fear, to life's lattermost minute;
I feel well assured — heaven shield me from harm! —
That jacket of blue had the d—ickens within it.

MRS. PARTINGTON'S FAREWELL,

WHEN SHE LEFT HER POST.

By the open door she stood,
And a drop stood in her eye, —
A thousand thronging memories
Restrained the sad good-by;
'T was sundering the golden chain
That long had bound her here,
And she gave to olden happiness
The tribute of a tear.

At last the word was uttered,
The farewell word was spoke;
Her eyes were dim with sorrow, part,
And part with coffee smoke;
She waved her hand and handkerchief,
A flush was on her brow,
And tremulously murmured she,
"I'll make my essex now!"

Then closed the door behind her,
She pensive moved and slow;
She lingered long upon the stairs, —
Ah, loth was she to go!
But her destiny was written,
She could bide no longer here,
And Mrs. Partington did weep
Full many a bitter tear!

WITHERED GRASS.

Like the still surface of the little lake,
  The heart is ruffled by the merest breath;
A word, a look, a flower, will oft awake
  A crowd of memories from their seeming death.

And late a simple tuft of faded grass
  Did rustle o'er my heart-strings with a tone
Of old affection which had slept, alas!
  Since the blest object of that love had flown.

My mind recalled therein the image fair
  Of her who bound the flowers in all their pride,
But who, more frail than summer blossoms are,
  Bowed her fair head, and in her spring-time died.

I lived again the love-illumined hours,
  When sweet communion cast around its spell,
Beneath the arches of those fragrant bowers,
  Adorned with roses that she loved so well.

Anew her smile made bright the hastening day,—
  How fleet it flew with Annie by my side!—
Her eye beamed on me with its olden ray,
  Her cheek still blushed in youth and beauty's pride.

Her voice once more its tender music poured
  Upon my eager, all-attentive ear,
And every syllable, of old adored,
  My listening spirit bowed itself to hear.

Her little hand sought mine, in beauteous trust;
  Her rounded cheek was pressed against my own;
Alas! remembrance turns the hand to dust,
  The rounded cheek in memory lives alone;—

Until the veil dividing us is riven,
  When, roaming on that bliss-environed plain,
To our enfranchised spirits it is given
  To join in loved companionship again.

E'en though an angel's crown adorn her head,
  Though bliss ecstatic be around her cast,
I can but deem the love once on me shed
  Is constant still, enduring to the last.

MEMORIES.

SING me the simple ballad strain
That pleased my heart in days of yore,
When earth seemed void of care and pain,
And all was bright my way before, —
Whose music, like the dews of night
That cheer the heart of summer flowers,
Checked youthful passion's fiery might,
And gave to virtue nobler powers.

Although a devious sea of years
Hath rolled its griefs and toils between, —
Although the present scene appears,
(And we ourselves), not what has been, —
Although the wrinkled brow betrays
The deeply-written trace of care,
And the bright hope of careless days
No longer finds a station there, —
Sing me the song that once you sung,
While I sit waiting at your knee,
The tones distilling from your tongue
Shall set my care-bound spirit free !
'T will wander through that distant past,
And revel mid those scenes again,
Known ere its sun was overcast
By aught of gloom or aught of pain ;

When innocence dwelt in the bowers,
  All consecrate to love and truth,
When life's new spring-light cheered the hours
  That made the calendar of youth.

Let others love the mightier strain,
  The brilliant gem of studied art;
O, let me hear that song again
  Whose melody first won my heart!

OUR ELLEN.

Ellen, Ellen, there 's no telling
  Half our love for thee, dear girl,
Features merry, lips like cherry,
  Sunny eye and glossy curl.

Ever singing, sweet voice ringing,
  Like a bird or like a bell,
Never weary, ever cheery,
  Ever striving to excel.

Late or early, never surly,
  Never fretting, seldom sad,
Thy appearing, always cheering,
  Everybody making glad.

Youth possessing, and each blessing
  Which the genial age imparts,
Still bewitching hall or kitchen,
  Ever reigning queen of hearts.

Always cheery, never dreary
  From the morn till setting sun,
Chicken feeding, playing, reading,
  Ever seasoning work with fun.

Cunning talker, agile walker,
  Bounding onward like a deer,
Blithesome moving, fair flowers loving,
  That brighter seem when thou art near.

Features merry, lips like cherry,
  Laughing eye and sunny curl,—
Ah, dear Ellen, there 's no telling
  Half our love for thee, dear girl!

PHILANTHROPOS AT FAULT.

All pensive walked the charcoalman
  His charcoal cart beside,
And plaintive was the tone in which
  His merchandise he cried;

And mournful was the look he cast
  Anon upon the ground,
And careless was the gaze he turned
  Upon the people round.

A gloom was resting on his brow,
  It trouble dire bespoke;
Adding a new and darker hue
  To clouds of charcoal smoke.

While all the world around was bright,
  And other hearts were glad,
Methought it was he walked alone
  Of all the people sad.

"Why sigh'st thou now, sad charcoalman?
  Why falls that bitter tear?
Is there no balm to ease thy grief?
  No soothing power near?"

Then calmly spoke the charcoalman,
  "I have n't any woes,
And that 'ere tear was sweat you saw
  A running down my nose;

"And I was thinking, very deep,
  That I was dry as sin,
And wondering how I 'd raise a drink,
  And had n't got the tin."

DOMESTIC JEWELS.

"These are my jewels," said the Roman dame,
  And laid her hand upon her children's tresses;
JEWELS! each mother's heart accepts the name, —
  How priceless held her beaming eye expresses.

The jewels of the queenly dame of Rome
  Are not confined to ancient musty story,
But gems as bright in many a quiet home
  Shed o'er its happiness a radiant glory.

There 's music in the infant's noisy glee,
  To ears attuned the songs of home to hear;
And childish laughter, jubilant and free,
  Makes glad the household's buoyant atmosphere.

King David, called a man of God's own heart, —
  And may his pious memory live forever! —
Pronounced him blest whose lot it was and part
  To have of children a full, bounteous quiver.

Amen! cry all true souls with ardent zest;
  And who that knows a thing will ever doubt them?
For, though but "troubles" they are oft confessed,
  Still home is very drear and sad without them.

THE LITTLE RIVULET.

I KNOW a gentle rill
That springs beside a hill,
  In the shade
Of the birch's emerald screen,
And the alder's cheerful green,
And the sweet fern in between,
Where the sun's bright glow, I ween,
  Ne'er hath strayed.

Down through the meadow wide,
Down by the deep wood-side,
Cheerfully its crystal tide
  Moves along;
And the cattle on its brink,
As they bow their heads to drink,
Seem to linger there and think
  On its song.

That song, — how sweet its notes,
As on the air it floats!
  And the birds,
On the willow spray that 's near,
Oft turn a raptured ear,
And stoop the bliss to hear
  Of its words.

The trees their branches wave,
As their roots the waters lave;
  And the grass
Receives a brighter hue,
And the flowers of gold and blue
Their brilliancy renew,
  As they pass.

And on its placid breast
The lilies fondly rest,
As if supremely blest
  With content;
And the sedges by its side
Look down upon its tide,
With love and trust and pride
  Sweetly blent.

And the living eddies twirl,
And their graceful ripples curl,
Like the tresses of a girl,
  And the sky
Sends troops of gorgeous clouds
To gaze on it in crowds,
  From on high.

Like the joyous tide of youth,
Like its virtue, like its truth,
Like its guilelessness and ruth,
  Sweetly gay,

Blessing all it glides among,
Cooling fevered brow and tongue,
Ever marked with smile and song,
  On its way.

And the gentle flow of song
Like its waters moves along,
Busy paths of men among,
  And its word,
Though the tempest din of life
Drown it, mayhap, in its strife,
Still its voice, with heaven rife,
  Shall be heard.

A VALENTINE.

Wife of mine — wife of mine —
Be thou still my Valentine;
Still, as when in Love's young day
We laughed the joyous hours away;
Still, as when on Life's broad stream
We launched our bark by Hope's bright beam;
Now, as then, my heart is thine, —
Thou art still my Valentine.

Wife of mine — wife of mine —
Thou art still my Valentine;
Though poor in purse, yet light in heart,
With sweet content we 'll never part;
No bickering strife nor jealous word
Shall in our humble courts be heard;
The day long and the night be mine,
To praise thee still, my Valentine.

Wife of mine — wife of mine —
Evermore my Valentine;
True happiness will always rest
Where Truth and Love have built their nest,

Where Virtue ever bright appears,
Undimmed, unmarked by changing years.
Such is the home thou 'st made of mine,
My old, my dearest Valentine.

Wife of mine — wife of mine —
Be thou still my Valentine;
The stream is broad, the tide is strong
That bears us on its breast along
Towards the shoreless, boundless sea,
Of a blest eternity;
My hopes of bliss round thee shall twine,
Eternally, my Valentine.

NEW HAMPSHIRE.

WRITTEN AS A CALL TO THE GATHERING OF THE SONS OF NEW HAMPSHIRE, IN 1852.

HARK! 't is New Hampshire's voice we hear,
But not in dread, as erst it spoke,
When trouble's clouds were hovering near,
And o'er her hills in terror broke.

When the fierce savage lit the flame
With hands dyed red in human life,
And mortal woe made loud acclaim
Amid the din of midnight strife.

Not now as when, with wrong oppressed,
Her heroes buckled on the sword,
Bared to their country's foes their breast,
And in its cause their life-blood poured.

Not now as when her battle peal
Gave fierce defiance to the foe,
And, right-impelled, the gleaming steel
Smote quick and strong the avenging blow.

Her summons ne'er was given in vain,—
An answering note from hill and glen
Echoed on many a battle plain,
In mighty deeds of gallant men.

The voice we hear breathes not of war,
  Nor aught of terror doth impart;
It tells no tale delight to mar,
  Nor thrills with anguished doubt the heart.

Like music notes that call to peace
  It bids us to her courts repair,
For one brief hour to find release
  From worldly strife and turmoil there.

To joy in memory of the past,
  To brush away the dust of years,
To bring back scenes too fair to last,
  Oft wakened with regretful tears;

And times when deeds of after date
  Were shadowed in each boyish plan,
Revealing in the child's estate
  The mighty promise of the man.

Mother! we hear thy kindly voice, —
  We fling discordant feelings by;
Brother with brother shall rejoice,
  And at thy summons gladly fly.

We pledge thee fondly, and the toast
  Each breast with warm emotion fills: —
"The good old state we love the most,
  Enthroned upon her thousand hills!"

OPENING OF THE LATE MR. JOHN SMITH'S WILL.

Or the evils of vagueness in specification, which the "writer" trusts may be avoided if ever a donation or legacy is meditated for him.

Now Mr. Smith, who had taken his leave,
  Was a prudentish sort of a man;
He always said to *prevent*, not retrieve,
  Was far the properest plan;
So, to hinder heart-burning and jealous hate
  And contending heirs make still,
Before he surrendered himself to fate
  He prudently framed a will.
But he kept it shut from mortal look,
  Nor could any define its tone;
To the favored *to-be* 'twas a close-sealed book,
  As well as the destined-to-none.
So hope ran strong and hope ran high
  In every degree of kin;
For virtues of Smith was breathed many a sigh,
  But smiles were reserved for his tin.

Nor wife nor child
On Smith had e'er smiled,
To inherit the money for which he had toiled;

And he 'd no nearer kin than uncles or cousins,
But these he had in numberless dozens.
Now cold was his clay,
And appointed the day
When his will was to open in legal way;
And the summons was put in the "Post," and all
Of the "next of kin" were invited to call
To see what share to their lot would fall;
And every heir
Had assembled there
From sea and land, and the Lord knows where:
    There was Smith from the plain,
      And Smith from the still,
    And Smith from the main,
      And Smith from the mill,
    And Smith from the mountain,
      And Smith from the mart,
    And Smith from the fountain,
      And Smith from the cart;
From the farthest off to the very near,
The Smiths all came the will to hear.

And they soberly sat
In neighborly chat,
Talking all about this and that,
While the clock near the door
Was watched more and more
As the minute-hand neared the hour of four—
The hour set when the opening seal
Their joy or their chagrin would reveal.

"Watch a pot and 't will never boil,"
Hasten time — 't is an up-hill toil;
Watch a clock for the hour to go,
'T is the weariest work a man can know;
And thus as they watched their patience waned,
Though not a voice of the mass complained,
For they thought it would n't be prudent to show
That they were aught anxious their doom to know.

Four struck at last, and, in eager array,
They gathered around an old man gray,
Who straightway out from its iron nook
Mr. Smith's very "last will" then took,
Nicely with black tape strongly tied,
With a huge black seal on either side.
The click of the shears, as the threads did part,
Went with a thrill to each waiting heart,
And then with anxious ear they hung
Upon every word from that old man's tongue.

His "soundness of mind"
And his creed were defined,
And then came the names to whom he was kind;
A cane to this,
And a box to that;
To one his dog,
Another his cat;
To this his buckles,
To this his hat;

Till, through the long list of legacies run,
The name of the heir was lighted upon;
When, in tones like the tones of a bell,
These were the words from his will that fell:—

"And further, I, John,
Have fixed upon,
To fill my place upon earth when I 'm gone,
John Smith the *tenth*, to be my heir,
My house to maintain and my honors to bear."

Now, here was a stew
To know what to do,
Or who the fortune had fallen to;
They could n't tell, were they to be shot,
For *fifteen* Johns were then on the spot;
And which was the tenth with the prefix "John"
They were sadly at loss to fix upon.
Then they argued the matter early and late,
But doubting grew with the growing debate.

And law-suits gathered, and fees flew free,
And juries tried it and could n't agree,
And fortunes were spent, till hope was gone,
In finding who was the favored *John!*
But they found instead that it *would n't pay*,
And so in court they allowed it to lay
In the dust and rust of years piled away.

A century is it since Mr. Smith died,
And his family name is scattered wide,

And towns have arisen upon his broad land,
Prosperity beaming on every hand;
A factory hums o'er his old hearth-stone,
But John Smith the *tenth one* was never known,
And John Smith's will will in chancery be,
Till Time is lost in Eternity's sea.

BENEVOLENCE.

A BENEVOLENT man was Absalom Bess, —
At each and every tale of distress
He blazed right up like a rocket;
He felt for all who 'neath poverty's smart
Were doomed to bear life's roughest part, —
He felt for them in his inmost heart,
But never felt in his pocket.

He did n't know rightly what was meant
By the Bible's promised four hundred per cent.
For charity's donation;
But he acted as if he thought railroad stocks,
And bonds secure beneath *earthly* locks,
Were better, with pockets brim full of rocks,
Than *heavenly* speculation.

Yet all said he was an excellent man;
For the poor he 'd preach, for the poor he 'd plan,—
To better them he was willing;
But the oldest one who had heard him pray,
And preach for the poor in a pitiful way,
Could n't remember, exactly, to say
He had ever given a shilling.

O, an excellent man was Absalom Bess,
And the world threw up its hands to bless,
  Whenever his name was mentioned;
But he died one day, he did, and O!
He went right down to the shades below,
Where all are bound, I fear, to go,
  Who are *only* good intentioned.

MIDNIGHT MUSIC.

SILENCE and darkness rested o'er the town;
 The midnight clock had tolled its solemn numbers,
When, like some blissful strain from heaven sent down,
 Broke music on the quiet of our slumbers.

Scarcely yet conscious, did the drowsy ear,
 Drinking in tones seraphic in their seeming,
Convey them to the soul entranced to hear,
 And wove them in the fabric of its dreaming.

Forgotten were the shadows of the night,
 And music shed a glory o'er the hour,
And sombre darkness grew with joy bedight,
 Beneath the influence of its magic power.

The infant, slumbering by its mother's breast,
 Waked at the sound, and waking smiled a blessing,
Then sank again serenely to its rest,
 Its tiny hand its mother's face caressing.

The sickness-bowed, to whom the weary time
 Lagged slowly on, replete with bitter sadness,
Heard the sweet note that filled the air, sublime,
 And felt a thrill run through his frame of gladness;

The fevered pulse a healthy tone assumed,
Harmonious throbbing to the music's measure,
And the glazed eye 'came transiently illumed
With radiant tokens of a present pleasure.

The widow's tears a moment ceased to flow;
She hailed the blessed melody a token
Of promise to her hopes, surcease from woe,
A note from spheres where unions are unbroken;

Bidding her heart its bitter strife to cease,
And from the future joyful hope to borrow;
Quelling the raging waves of grief to peace,
And soothing, like a charm, her preying sorrow.

To the close-curtained chamber of the bride
The music notes on airy wings ascended,
Blessed the fond pair harmoniously allied,
And with their aspirations sweetly blended.

But, all too soon did flee that 'witching strain, —
Fled 'mid the darkness, thus made doubly dreary;
And the still, solemn hours rolled on again
Their sluggish wave, more tedious and weary.

A SPRITELY REVENGE.

TENDER-hearted, list my ditty!
   Hear the tale of love I tell,
Tune your harps to notes of pity,
   Let your sighs responsive swell.

Polly Ann Matilda Wiggins,—
   O, so bright and fair was she!—
Lovéd Hezekiah Higgins,
   And was loved as well by he.

Naught but love, though, were they rich in,—
   Pewter lent their lives no charm,—
Polly toiléd in a kitchen,
   Hezekiah tilled a farm.

Now awaked the golden fever,
   Hezekiah took it bad;
Polly begged he would n't leave her,
   But the money must be had.

Matrimony waited on it—
   Neck or nothing—death or life—
And he vowed, by Polly's bonnet,
   Fortune gained, he 'd make her wife.

Praying, sighing, kissing, crying,
Hezekiah bade good-by;
Polly stood her tears a-drying,
With her apron to her eye.

Time rolled by, and, sad and lonely,
Tender Polly wept and prayed,
Got one little letter only,
For which forty cents she paid.

Disconsolate she grew and badly,
Vainly sighing for relief;
Then, by marrying Jim Hadley,
Flung herself away, in grief.

Hezekiah at the "diggins"
Took his pick and worked away,
Dreamed all night of Polly Wiggins,
Thought of Polly all the day.

But the fever went and took him,
As it many has beside,
And at last his breath forsook him, —
So, in consequence, he died.

And his spirit, homeward turning, —
Little cost to it, I ween, —
Straightway went where, love's flame burning,
Polly Wiggins last he 'd seen.

Sad, poor ghost, the way he found her!
  Tears his ghostly eyes bedim;
Hadley had his arm around her —
  She was smiling "sweet" on Jim.

Sorrow then gave way to anger,
  Knocked he with his spectral fist,
Till they started with the clangor,
  And their spirits quaked to list.

Knocked he, then, and tipped the table;
  Polly ran and screamed for fear,
Hadley cut as fast as able,
  Those unearthly knocks to hear.

Hadley cut and Polly wilted, —
  Well she knew the sounds of dread;
And the ghost of him she jilted
  Was most fully aveng-ed.

THE OLD GREEN COTTON.

My old green cotton "umberel,"
Thou 'st served me long and served me well,
And now it grieves my heart to tell
 That thou hast left me, —
That thievish hand, with purpose fell,
 Of thee has reft me.

Many 's the wet and dreary day
Thou 'st braved the perils of the way,
When lowering tempests made essay
 To soak me through;
Thou 'st dared the elemental fray,
 As good as new.

Relentless man! us two to part, —
Was there no softness in thy heart,
No voice from out its depths to start,
 Thy hand to stay?
A fiend — a very fiend — thou art, —
 'T is plain as day.

But may no comfort on thee rest!
May all thy airs, that should be west,

Blow from the east with furious zest,
    Thy joy to ban!
May conscience render thee unblest,
    A wretched man!

Round thee may raging rain-storms roar,
And thunder threaten vengeance sore!
May that old umberel no more
    Protection shed!
May heaven its rain relentless pour
    Upon thy head!

OWED TO MONEY.

Of dollars we 're dreaming, for dollars striving,
The only object of worth in life ;
The mind of man, for his greed contriving,
Dares the encounter of every strife.

The silvery stream all mankind follow,
Wherever its meanderings run,
Whose course is lit by the shining dollar,
Brighter and warmer than noonday sun.

Everywhere is this dollar gleaming,
Everywhere in church or in mart,
And, like bright rays of sunshine, streaming
Through every chink of the human heart.

Mighty the power in money that dwelleth,—
There is no potentate like to this;
Its triumphs the history of ages telleth,
'T is the key to every earthly bliss.

It opens the door of the poet's vision,
It smooths the path of the good and brave,
It blunts the arrows of man's derision,
It lightens the bonds of the fettered slave.

Most potent soother of human anguish,
  Everywhere its power is shown,
Upraising those who in misery languish,
  Easing woes that the heart may own.

The stings of love are alleviated,
  Broken hearts are made good as new,
Old cheerfulness is reinstated,
  The true made better, the false made true.

By rail-car crashing, furious dashing,
  Husband 's struck from the roll of life;
A law-suit follows — ten thousand dollars
  Consoles the inconsolable wife.

Character 'neath the tongue of scandal
  Black is made as the shades of night;
Let the dollar gleam, like a mighty candle,
  The clouds of gloom are put to flight.

Dollars! dollars! — *the* song and *the* story,
  The genius of man has e'er sung or said;
Old painters, with just ideas of glory,
  Drew golden hoops round each holy head.

O, money, money! all men adore thee,
  An altar thou hast in every heart;
E'en virtue's power must fail before thee,
  In robbing woe of its keenest smart.

Henceforward money be my endeavor;
  Shut, eyes and heart, to all beside!
Gold to my progress shall prove the lever,
  And silver dollars be deified.

Hurra for money! old virtues vanish, —
  Friendship and love that once controlled, —
Such common stars the world must banish,
  Whose guiding star is a star of gold.

A VISION OF LIFE.

Amid the troubled fancies of my dreaming,
There rose a vision radiant and bright,
A world of sadness from its gloom redeeming,
And shedding on my path a blessed light.

An angel boy to my embrace was given,
On whom my heart poured lavishly its love:
I felt he was a blessing sent from heaven —
An emanation from the home above.

In his dark eyes my love saw its reflection,
His voice like music thrilled me with its tone,
His tender arms, in confident protection,
Entwined in fond conjunction with my own.

His kiss! I feel it on my lip yet glowing,
As when his cheek unto my own I prest,
And my full heart, with tenderness o'erflowing,
Its great, its boundless happiness confessed.

And day by day I marked his mind's expansion,
  A growing love I saw that met my own;
I thought not of the frailty of the mansion
  Where his fair spirit had set up its throne.

There came a cloud across my dream, of sorrow,
  And pain, and misery, and dying strife,
And effort vain from human aid to borrow,
  To keep alive the beam we know as life.

The heavenly vision fled, and gloom succeeding
  Arrayed my soul in bitterness of woe;
There seemed no solace for my heart left bleeding—
  No voice to bid my tears to cease their flow.

No voice! ah, yes, my drooping spirit heareth
  A word of joy, as if an angel spake:
The accent glad my saddened soul now cheereth,
  And all its crushed and wounded powers awake.

It saith, the Mighty One who gave the blessing
  Has called it, pure and holy, to his side;
Freed it from woes and cares of earth, oppressing,
  To live for aye in joys beatified;—

That this dark cloud, called death, that closed my vision,
  Is but the mist that hides from me the sun;
And living yet, in atmosphere elysian,
  My boy awaits till my short race be run;—

That love burns brighter, in that realm eternal,
  Enkindled in this care-bound world of ours—
Borrowing new strength, 'mid those pure airs supernal,
  To bless us once again in heavenly bowers.

Blest is our faith, the mists of death dispelling,
  And heavenly hope, that looks within the veil!
Bright lights to guide us until, these excelling,
  Our faith and hope in glad fruition fail.

AN OLD PARABLE MODERNIZED.

THE Pharisee stands, with outspread hands,
  And eyes turned up in prayer,
In his cushioned pew, broadly in view,
  That people may see him there;
And good people praise his devotional air,
And his condescension their praise to share.

But the humble one feels his dark sins roll
  Like a wave o'er his bosom's peace;
Ill, ill at rest, he smites his breast,
  And prays that his strife may cease;
"God be merciful — extend thine arm,
Save me, a sinner, from impending harm!"

And the God that reads the heart that pleads
  Shall bless to that humble soul
A measure of peace that shall never cease
  O'er life its blest control;
Nor shall pride or self-trust obtain the goal,
Alone to be gained by the humble soul.

LINES IN AN ALBUM.

I 'M sad that I don't know you, Miss, nor how you think
  or look,
No more than you the stranger one who thus profanes
  your book;
So of course I cannot praise you much, whatever I may
  say,
Avoiding thus the odiousness of flattery in my lay.
But you 'll still be my inspirer, as in tales of old romance,
When many a knightly pennon waved from many a battle
  lance, —
When knightly vows were given oft, upheld by sword
  and mace,
Of fealty to dames of straw, who 'd ne'er revealed their
  face, —
And I, like these old chevaliers, devote my pen to you,
And act as if your wish and will your votary fully knew.
Write! is the mandate, and at once my muse has spread
  her wing,
And this, the trophy of her flight, she to your feet doth
  bring:

WOMAN.

Thine is the power to make the arid plain
  Glow bright in sweet affection's genial ray,
  And, twining roses round man's troubled way,
Bring him, though lost, to Eden's joys again.

His fall becomes his bliss, for to his grief
 Thy soothing influence, perpetual, brings
 A balm, like dew from night's o'ershadowing wings,
Cheering his toil-bowed heart with blest relief.
Without thee! — Heaven knew man's direst need,
 And thee, sweet ministering angel, sent,
 With earthly and with heavenly feelings blent,
To heal the heart that otherwise might bleed.
Thy spirit brightens life's care-clouded vale,
And guides him hopeful where he else might fail.

'Tis but a simple tale I sing, — of small poetic worth;
Soar we to heaven as we may, our thoughts come back to earth —
For though woman's angel nature might claim that upper sphere,
Her better portion is to bless the sad and sorrowing here.

A GLANCE OUT INTO THE COOL.

"And a' babbled of green fields."

A BURNING sun above is gleaming,
And, as we bask beneath its ray,
The yearning fancy, in its dreaming,
Wandereth from the town away;

Wandereth to the dim recesses,
Out in the old wood's spreading shade,
Where the cool circling air e'er blesses,
Where the hot sunbeams ne'er have strayed;

To where the pine-trees' mournful breathing
Lures the mind to peaceful themes,
Like voice of some good spirit, wreathing
Heaven's sweet cadence with its dreams;

To where, remote from habitation,
Within a deep and rocky dell,
O'erarching trees, in exultation,
Guard in their shade the little well,

That through the rocky chancel stealeth,
With a low-murmuring song of bliss,
Till brighter blooms the flower that feeleth
The inspiration of its kiss;

To where lone paths, 'neath sombre shadows,
Court to romantic haunts away,
Where purling brooks, in emerald meadows,
Glow lovely in the light of day;

To where bright birds the morn awaken,
Greeting its coming with their lays,
And, with a joyousness unshaken,
Make glad the whole long summer days;

To where old Ocean, wildly dashing,
Pours its broad flood upon the shore,
The mighty volume thundering, crashing,
Speaks freedom in its awful roar;

To where deep lakes, mid lofty mountains,
Shine back upon the summer sky,
Where icy rills, from secret fountains,
The flower-decked path come trickling by,—
Trickling o'er sands of pearly whiteness,
Pouring their treasures at his feet,
Tempting the eye with crystal brightness,
Tempting the lips with waters sweet.

But, like the artist, whose creation
He worshipped as a thing divine,
So we, in Nature's contemplation,
Yearn to do homage at her shrine.

Away, vain phantom! fond illusion,
Waking discontent and doubt!
Say, what to him is this profusion,
Who, like Sterne's starling, "can't get out."

THE OLD BACHELOR'S BEQUEST.

SHOWING HOW AN OLD BACHELOR WAS BROUGHT TO HIS SENSES BY THE SOFTENING INFLUENCE OF RHEUMATISM.

Old Roger lay groaning in bitter pain,
  Alone in his chamber high;
From early morn he'd unheeded lain,
  And the time dragged wearily by.

No kindly hands or voices were there,
  To soothe his bitter woe;
No friendly step pressed his chamber stair,
  A sympathy to show.

His old watch whispered the waning day,
  As it hung above his head,
And phials and potions, in grim array,
  Were ranged beside his bed.

Alone! How sad is the word *alone!*
  How sad alone to feel!
Where the drear hours give no welcome tone,
  Nor one kind look reveal.

Then, as he groaned, a sudden thought,
  Like a ray of blessed light,
Illumined his mind, with sadness fraught,
  And put his gloom to flight.

"I 'll make my will," said he to himself,
  "And, though I 've no lands to give,
I 'll give what is better than earthly pelf,
  The secret of how to live.

"I 'll give advice that shall gladden life,
  And make it more pleasantly glide;
The young man I 'll counsel to marry a wife,
  And the maiden to be a bride,

"That, when the long days of sickness press,
  They may not, like me, be alone,
But gentle hearts be near, to bless,
  And affection's gentle tone;

"Each wish be watched with a tender care,—
  Where loving ones shall bring
A charm to surround the sufferer there,
  That will blunt affliction's sting.

"Perchance the hour by childhood's voice
  May be with music filled,
Till the lagging pulse at the tone rejoice,
  That before was nearly stilled.

"No wife,—no child! I have lived in vain,
  And I feel my error keen;
O! could I renew my life again,
  A wiser I'd be, I ween."

THE GARDEN GRAVES.

A country family grave-yard is an interesting object, always, where a small precinct is sacredly reserved as the resting-place of the departed, and consecrated by affectionate memory. It becomes a home object, and mingles with the things of home, from its familiarity rendering death less terrible, and smoothing the way that leads to renewed companionship with the departed. In Newington, N. H., is a spot of this description, a community of graves in a flower-garden ; the beautiful things of earth blooming among them, and the air above them filled with fragrance.

Room for the household graves amid the flowers!
  Room for the young and pure,
  Whose spirits shall endure,
While fade away earth's perishable bowers.

Gentle were they in life, those cherished dead!
  And hope's effulgent ray
  Shone brightly on their way,
While innocence its charm around them shed.

But brightest seasons soon are overcast;
  The cloud swept by in gloom,
  And to an early tomb
Have goodness, youth and beauty, hither passed.

The infant, smiling, sank beneath the lid;
  The youth with kindling thought,
  The maiden, beauty-fraught,
And all are in the garden graves here hid.

'T is meet they mingle with the flowrets bright,—
  With the fair things of earth,—
  For from their very birth
Did they, like sweet flowers, shed around delight.

And here can fancy turn, as seasons fly,
  And in each floral gem
  Imagine traits of them
Reflected in the earth from realms on high.

A consecrated shrine becomes the spot;
  A holy bliss is shed
  About their lowly bed,
That ever-changing time shall deaden not.

They are *not* dead, but sleeping 'mid the flowers!
  To wake to life where gloom
  Finds in its sphere no room,
As in this sorrow-burdened world of ours.

Can we call Death a messenger of woe,
  Where with his glad release
  He gives the mortal peace?
A hopeful faith, responsive, answers No.

Since writing the foregoing lines, the one at whose suggestion they were composed has been added to the number gathered within that silent community among the flowers, — a fit receptacle for one beloved for beauties of character that had long marked her for the higher sphere to which she has since been called.

Naught is too sacred for the touch of Death,
And she, the radiant one,
Whom love so leaned upon,
Has felt the mildew of his blighting breath.

She died when flowers were opening to the sun,
When germs threw by the earth,
And sprang in joy to birth,
Their brief but beauteous destiny to run.

Thus her bright spirit fled its cumbering clay;
Born to a higher life,
Where misery nor strife
Shall mar the glory of its endless day.

They laid her by her mates amid the flowers,
And ne'er did dust more blest
Pass to its tranquil rest,
Nor fairer spirit seek celestial bowers.

And kindly will the flowers their perfume fling,
And birds with music rare
Make eloquent the air
Above the bed where they, the loved, lie slumbering.

THE 'BIDING CURSE.

Roofless and dreary the old pile has stood,
  For many a weary year,
And it seemeth no home for aught of good,
  But a haunt of gloom and fear.

The bricks are crumbling one by one,
  And the windows widely ope,
And sickly plants unguided run,
  And round the dark walls grope.

And children avoid it in their play,
  As 't were a thing of fright;
Alone it stands in the glare of day,
  And alone in the hush of night.

And the door-sills are rotting the doors away,
  Though they ne'er by foot are prest,
And the spider holds unchallenged sway,
  With no hand to molest.

And the spout hangs faint by a feeble nail,
  And it utters a doleful cry,
As it feels the force of the passing gale,
  Like one in his agony.

How ghastly and white the moonbeams play
  Around the old pile drear!
And the passer hastens upon his way,
  With a feeling of pressing fear.

For the moonbeams white and the still midnight,
  And the weakness of his heart,
Lead him to dread that elf or sprite
  May out from the portal start.

Ah! the bitter curse that the old man spoke
  Is working its mission fell,
And the spirit of dread he dared invoke
  Has woven his baleful spell.

Nor prayers nor tears nor holy years
  May move that fearful ban,
Where Desolation its form uprears,
  And laughs at the fears of man.

And where is the beautiful Geraldine now,
  With her wealth of golden hair,—
And her eye of mirth, that made that hearth
  With paradise compare?

And where is the sordid wretch so cold,
  Who won the charming maid,
And, all for the sake of her father's gold
  Her guileless heart betrayed?

Gone — all gone — and the glad home gone —
Decay on its hearthstone reigns;
The insatiate grave hath claimed its own,
But the living curse remains.

"That old house, there? Why, sir, you dream,
That 'ere 's a 'stillery old!
You may read on the fence, by the bright moonbeam,
That to-morrow 't is to be sold."

Thus fades! — O, plague on the plodding elf
That dared my dream profane;
I 'll lay me by on some quiet shelf,
And try to dream again.

THE OLD IMAGE-MAKER.

Busily toileth, the whole day long,
  The image-maker his works among;
His eye from his labor is never away,
  And he plies his toil with a silent tongue.

Varied and strange his creations appear,
  From the gay and bright to the dull and sad;
And every image is moulded here,
  As the maker's fancy is gloomy or glad.

Here Innocence stands in her holiest form,
  Her brow illumed with heaven's own ray;
Here Hope smiles sweetly mid sorrow's storm,
  And points the true to a happier day.

And Love appeareth as erst he seemed,
  Ere blinded and stifled with sordid dust,
When warm in his ray the young heart beamed,
  Unmarred by doubt and undimmed by lust.

Here is Youth, with the glow of hopeful pride,
  Impatiently waiting for man's estate,
To fling himself on the moving tide,
  And sink or swim in the stream of Fate.

Here is Ambition and early Fame;
  Here serpent Sin in many a fold,
With tongue of poison and eye of flame,
  And glittering scales of burnished gold.

Here Grief is beheld, and her swollen eye
  Drops sadly a tear for her darling dead;
How more for the *living*, who cannot die,
  Should those sad tears of Grief be shed!

Thus ever forms he the sad and bright —
  Living again 'neath his master hand;
Leading captive the feeling and sight,
  Like the fabled sway of a magic wand.

That image-maker is Memory true,
  Working deep in the minds of men;
And acts and feelings of every hue,
  Or pleasant or sad, have life again.

WELCOME TO JENNY LIND.

WHEN Genius strikes her loftiest note,
  O, wide is its vibration, Jenny!
It sounds through lands the most remote,
  Where worth wakes admiration, Jenny;

An universal meed its claim,
  Its province earth's wide limit, Jenny;
Its glory spreadeth like a flame,
  And Death alone may dim it, Jenny.

Thy praise hath swept across the sea,
  Our hearts are won already, Jenny;
All heads, elate to think on thee,
  Are far from being steady, Jenny.

From east, and west, and south, and north,
  We hear the same note rising, Jenny,
Heralding thy rare virtues forth,
  And loveliness surprising, Jenny.

All breezes waft the theme along,
  In every clime it 's sounded, Jenny;
For all men fealty pay to song,
  In lands, "however bounded," Jenny.

We prize thee for thy merits bright,
  Thy heart's warm flow of pity, Jenny;
Ten thousand tongues, with wild delight,
  Cry welcome to our city, Jenny.

We greet thee with a cordial cheer,
  And bless thy smile so winning, Jenny;
Each heart beats glad that thou art here,
  And each man's head 's a spinning, Jenny!

SPIRIT LONGING.

Forever wakefully the ear is turning
 To catch some token from the shadowy sphere;
Forever is the full heart strongly yearning
 Some word of promise from its depths to hear.

When the dark shadows flit along the ceiling,
 As the dull firelight trembles in the grate,
Fancy, fond yet with old remembered feeling,
 Striveth the loved and lost to re-create.

It feels their presence in the hush of even,
 When day's excitement settles to repose;
It sees them in the twilight hues of heaven,
 And in the beauties that the stars disclose.

It heeds the breezes that around are playing,
 And in their music fain that voice would hear,
Whose melody it deems may yet be straying,
 To glad the faithful hearts yet sorrowing here.

When midnight, resting like a pall above us,
  Within its dusky arms enfoldeth all,
We list for those whom hope says still may love us,
  And sigh as their unanswering names we call.

We dream, and ever-faithful memory bringeth
  Old happiness we may not know awake;
The rose of pleasure in our pathway springeth,
  And rills of joy where we our thirst may slake.

But, O, returning consciousness dispelleth
  The sweet illusion in whose thrall was bliss,
And strife renewed in life's encounter quelleth
  Regrets, as we our dreams of joy dismiss!

And are there kindred spirits dwelling by us,
  And mingling yet their loving thoughts with ours,
Forever drawing in communion nigh us,
  In virtue's way to cheer our lagging powers?

O, are there voices that may, at our asking,
  Come to assure us of that better state,
Where, evermore in endless pleasures basking,
  Those gone before our fond reünion wait?

The seeking soul asks for prophetic vision
  To penetrate the dark, mysterious cloud
That intervenes between the land elysian
  And this dull earth, where sins and sorrows crowd.

The grave is not a bourn whose sombre portal
Closeth eternal o'er the bright and fair,
But through its gate to blessedness immortal
The spirit passeth, endless life to share.

Still old affection hereward back is turning,
And whispering words to us of joy and peace,
And spiritual eyes are round us burning
With holier love as heavenly powers increase.

A SWEET REVENGE.

It is a glorious privilege that a poor fellow, without a cent in his pocket, enjoys, to pitch into the rich with a will, without a fear of being hit back. The following may be of this spirit ; but, alas ! there is much in the world to warrant the belief in its truth. We have adapted the title of the poem to the above idea.

There lived a man, — no matter where or when, —
A man of note and mightiness was he ;
He bore control among his fellow-men,
And wealthy was on land and on the sea.

He houses reared, and lived in grand estate, —
Had servants trembling wait for his command ;
His heart with vast possession was elate,
And honors thickly pressed on every hand ;

And white-winged ships rushed far to do his will,
And men were toiling for him in the mart ;
His word could loose the wheels of many a mill,
His mandate cause the streams of trade to start.

Withdrawn his smile, and banks refused their aid;
  Frowned he, and happy faces anxious grew;
A potentate within the realm of trade,
  One only motive in his life he knew :

He lived for money, — bartered all for dross, —
  No holier motive moved his sordid soul;
His only fear was wakened for its loss, —
  His only knowledge lay in its control.

And thus he lived. Benevolence ne'er shone,
  In one blest act, to mark his selfish way ;
No pity smiled in him, that might atone
  For avarice there which held unceasing sway.

But equal fate, at last, ends rich and poor!
  Disease, that knows not station, bowed him down;
The rich man's wealth could not its lord secure
  From ills that fall in anguish on the clown.

He died. The grave closed o'er his hoary head,
  And lying marble gleamed above the sod,
On which the passing scoffer sneering read,
  "An honest man 's the noblest work of God."

Yet, further than earth's narrow bounds we go, —
  To man the power of prophecy is given ;
He sees that soul, so proud in wealth below,
  Of mean account among the hosts of heaven.

The beggars of the earth who sought his aid,
  And turned unpitied from his door away,
Stand in those heavenly courts in light arrayed,
  Where his weak vision may not dare to stray.

Too late he mourns facilities misspent,
  As retrospect his life-chart doth unroll;
He sees that adding earthly cent to cent
  Was forging fetters for his weary soul.

PARSON STORER IN A FIX; OR, THE MAGIC OF A KISS MISAPPLIED.

An austere planet ruled the hour when Parson S. had birth,
The veriest crab that ever backward crawled upon the earth;
All worldly loves and worldly lights he reckoned but a sham,
And, though his calling was to save, he would much rather damn.
Stern rigor dwelt within his eyes, naught kindly there was seen,—
Severity was written plain in all his sombre mien;
The urchins slunk his path away and glanced at him awry,
Their marbles unregarded lay while he was passing by;
The dogs would stop their barking and demurely walk away,
As they saw his eye upon them, would "Sweetheart, Blanche and Tray."

A joke he called frivolity,—a quiz was aye his bane,
A joyous laugh he'd sadly hope he'd never hear again;

It was said he hanged a puppy-dog that once had dared
to play
And frolic round his study floor upon a Sabbath day.

O, how he frowned the custom down where girls and lads
would meet,
And sourer than verjuice he to hear their kisses sweet!
He wanted courtship godly done, — a special service
writ, —
The ways that nature had prescribed he did n't like a
bit.

Now, the parson had a servant-maid, — a little charming
girl,
Her face was graced by many a smile, her head by many
a curl;
Her eye was blue as heaven, and like a bird's her voice,
A glance of which, a tone of which, made many a heart
rejoice;
Her heart was always spring-light and all devoid of care,
And everybody wondered how it chanced that she came
there.

If Parson Storer chided her, she heeded not a grain,
But her voice soon sounded cheerily around the house
again;
'T would echo through the parsonage, through gallery
and room,
Till the ancient pile was robbed *per force* of half its som-
bre gloom.

Now, Susan — that 's her name — had a lover true and kind,
But to follow by the parson's rule they never were inclined;
The kitchen fire saw many a scene that, had the parson kenned,
Would have furnished texts for homilies and sermons without end.

When the light had left the parson's room, an hour after prayers,
And many an hour after that, was brightly burning theirs;
And kisses sweet and many, and many a tender word,
Had the clock that stood behind the door both witnessèd and heard.

O, love! thou art delicious when dressed in sauce like this!
I often think 't were well to stop at this way-house to bliss,
For wear and tear of after years must sprinkle in alloy,
Which ardent lovers never know in plenitude of joy.

It was on the night of Saturday, and the parson's light was out,
And Susan — bright, expecting Sue — was bustling about;
With eager eye she marked the door, with eager ear the lock,
Awaiting anxiously to hear the music of that knock.

At last, her patience wholly spent, she looked out on the night;
The moon had sunk behind the hills, the stars were dimly bright,
She listened long to hear the step that she was wont to hear,
When a hand upon the outer gate gave rapture to her ear.

Upon the wings of love she flew (don't think of earthly feet!
'T is vulgar, such a medium, where ardent lovers meet);
She clasped the comer in her arms, she hung upon his breast,
As captured bird would cling restored unto its natal nest;
And kisses shed she on his lips, — her words outgushing fast, —
"Bless you, Samuel, my dear, and have you come at last?"

"Susan, what means this?" gently spoke the parson's heavy tone,
For it was he, and no one else, out in the night alone;
And sore surprised was he to feel the ardor thus bestowed,
But his breast experienced a flame that never there had glowed.

And Parson Storer grew a man of better mould from then,
And acted out a better part among his fellow-men;

And people talked, as oft they will, and shoulders they
did shrug,
And laid his new-found gentleness to pretty Susan's hug.

And Susan married happily, and fortune's sunny rays
Smiled on her and her children for many, many days;
And oft has she the story told, with ever new delight,
Of how she hugged the parson there upon that summer
night.

THE COTTAGE BY THE SEA.

THERE 's a lonely cottage that stands by the sea,
A dreary old pile to view ;
The winds howl around it most dismally,
And whistle its crannies through.

The salt spray whitens its walls of clay,
And gleams in its roof of thatch,
And the swallows build in its chimney gray,
And their young in quiet hatch.

T is here the hardy fisherman dwells, —
The fisherman bold and free ;
He knows the tale that the bluff wind tells,
And the whisperings of the sea.

He reads the stars, like a book, by night ;
And the bright auroral rim,
That arches the north with its mystical light,
Has a meaning deep to him.

The tides that flow and the winds that blow,
  And the sea-birds on the wing,
And the clouds that rise in the changing skies,
  To him all wisdom bring.

He launches his boat on the heaving wave,
  Where, far down its crystal deep,
The ocean's tenants in freedom lave,
  Or in peaceful shallows sleep.

He casts his line where the fishes shine,
  In the breast of the generous sea;
And he utters a prayer, — "O, motherly Mer,
  Be bountiful unto me!"

And the motherly sea her stores unseals,
  And she gives with a ready hand;
More lavish and free are the fruits of the sea
  Than the yield of the sluggish land.

There 's the fisherman's waiting wife at home,
  And the fisherman's boys and girls,
And that little one, who will laughingly run,
  To kiss him through her curls.

Then his boat glides over the yielding spray,
  As he bends to the ashen oar;
And his quick ear hears, from afar away,
  A welcoming cry from the shore.

Thus the fisherman lives most happy and free,
Nor other wealth doth crave
Than the blessing of love and his liberty,
And the product of the wave.

No palace of wealth, with gorgeous state,
No castle of high degree,
Contains a joy more pure or great
Than the cottage by the sea.

ON THE DEATH OF A CHILD.

"Is it well with the child? And she answered, It is well."

How fondly to their little charge they clung,
   Nor deemed the spoiler near, with cruel skill
To chill in silence that melodious tongue,
   Whose gentle note had made their heart-strings thrill,
Blessing their home with the sweet influence shed
   From the rich treasure of a child's full love,
And the quick moments, as they onward sped,
   Filling with rapture equalled but above!

Hard is the blow that sunders love like this,—
   The bleeding heart rebels when thus 't is riven;
So long a feaster on its borrowed bliss,
   It grudges what is gathered back to heaven;
Crushed and despairing in its night of grief,
   It cannot see the hand that wields the rod,
But reason's light will come to its relief,
   And show the dealing of a righteous God.

Then time will strew around that little grave
   Perennial roses, endless in their bloom,
And memory, faithful memory, shall save
   All that was lovely from that early tomb;

The pain, the misery of the dying child
   Will be forgotten in the distant days,
While every look of love that on them smiled
   Will be revealed to retrospection's gaze.

Its image, printed deep within the heart,
   Reflected in the air, the tree, the flower,
Shall richest comfort to the last impart,
   Till closes life's short, perishable hour.
Then, brighter than when on the earth it smiled,
   'T will beckon onward to the world of rest;
Blest region! where the parent and the child
   May find reünion 'mongst the immortal blest.

THE TABLES TURNED: A DOGGEREL.

Or how Alderman Jones saw things in a dream which may go to account for the repeal of the dog law.

THE sad nineteenth* had come and passed,
And many a fair cur breathed its last
Beneath fell blows and cruel licks
From urchins armed with oaken sticks,
Or huge men waiting but the word
To murder all the canine herd.
The law to back them, small they cared,
But pug and poodle equal fared,
And sturdy bull-dogs, terriers, setters,
Were stilled in death's unyielding fetters,
And headless lay as still as clods,
Let owners see them, hang the odds!
O, 't was a horrid, frightful slaughter,
And all Cochituate's pure water
Can from fair Boston ne'er efface
This record of her dire disgrace.

That night saw Alderman Jones in bed,
A warm wool nightcap on his head,

* On the 19th of April, 18—, the law went into effect authorizing the killing of all dogs, at large, not muzzled.

And, tucked in snug, he lay reposing,—
Sweet Mrs. J. beside him dozing!
The night had passed till twelve and over,
When blackest shadows o'er us hover,
When "church-yards yawn," and ghosts and devils
And other kidney make their revels.

'T is best to be in bed by nine,
With conscience undisturbed, like mine;
Then sleep will seal your eyelids weary,
And all your dreams be bright and cheery;
But Mr. Jones, inclined to royster,
Had that night taken one more oyster
Than was his usual habit fixed,
And forty drops of brandy, mixed
With "aqua pura" just to soften
The ill of drinking water often;
And troubled images perplexing,
Soul-harrowing and wild and vexing,
Came up within his mind while sleeping,
That set his very flesh all creeping;
His hair arose on end like bristles,
And fancy showered on him thistles
That stung and burned him as he lay,
From which he could not get away.
The sweat ran down his sides like rain,—
He tossed and turned and turned again,
Till Mrs. Jones, her patience shaken,
Strove her fast-sleeping spouse to waken,

And on the word, as soon as spoke,
He started up, — the spell was broke.
He rubbed his eyes — he looked affrighted —
Till on his wife his glance alighted,
Then spoke, in tones with horror filled,
"Call off the dogs, or I am killed!"

A shake or two from Mrs. J.
Dispelled the mists that round him lay,
When, rousing to a lucid state,
He told the dream I here relate:

He thought that by some high decision
Man's power was brought into derision,
And in one little, fleeting hour
He was deposed, and dogs had power,
To prove the antiquated say
That every "dog should have his day."
Reversed was everything in town, —
The dogs went up the men went down,
And every station and estate,
That man had occupied of late,
Was handed o'er to canine rule,
In hall and cottage, mart and school;
In doctor's chair and pulpit high
The dogs were placed their skill to try;
A big dog filled the judge's seat,
In wig and fixings all complete,
And jury dogs, like human brothers,
Sat listening to the tales of others;

And, what to Jones seemed very strange,
Many scarcely marked the change,
Accustomed they so long before
To see them filled by little more.
And canine councils gravely scanned
The works the tyrant man had planned,
Devoutly thankful kindly fate
Had called them in to save the state.

Then time went by, and they detected
That man by madness was infected, —
That dread of water was the sign
By which the malady to define, —
And straightway, for their own protection,
They passed a law to stay the infection:
That every man who water dreaded
Should first be caught and then beheaded,
Unless he wore a muzzle snug
Around his brandy-branded mug,
And every one who passed for man
Was reckoned fitting for the ban;
Then men walked round with leathern straps
Upon their mouths, or wire traps,
Or some device their masters picked
A kindly misery to inflict.

Alas for those who went unguarded!
Their rashness was with stripes rewarded:
Official dogs, with iron teeth,
Soon worried, hurried them to death,

And fifty cents a head was given
For those which were n't worth half when living;
And mangled forms lay scattered round,
Headless and marked by many a wound;
And taunts of sausages and pies,
Like human ribald, did arise,
Till it was hard to choose the best,
The canine or the human jest.

Then men grew timid in their state;
Soon changed was tone and step elate,
And humble were the high and proud,
The biggest of the human crowd.

An alderman ran from a puppy's bark,
A huge policeman hid his mark,
And broke his switch at a small dog's growl,
As he raced down street with a horrid howl;
And Jones's self, while his breath did fail,
Was chased with a tin pot tied to his tail,
And a big dog tried were he mad, with a wink,
By offering him some water to drink!
This was going too far for a joke,
And glad was he when at last he awoke,
And the sequel was that his dire affright
Kept him awake the live-long night.

THE MISER.

No more doth the miser count his gold
  By the lamp's uncertain ray;
Nor brings he it from that hidden hold
  Where years it hath lain away.

No cumbrous bars of the oaken wood,
  No walls of the granite stone,
Needeth he now to preserve that good
  Which once was his care alone.

He soundly sleeps in his midnight bed,
  Nor feareth he for his pelf;
No loaded pistols are 'neath his head,
  No daggers near on the shelf.

He trembles no more at the watchman's tread,
  As he paceth his nightly round;
And he quakes not with that olden dread
  At the least mysterious sound.

But a shrewd old fellow he grows each day,
  And has found, to his heart's content,
That better than packing of dollars away
  Is the grateful cent per cent.

THE MISER.

No more doth the miser count his gold
   By the lamp's uncertain ray;
Nor brings he it from that hidden hold
   Where years it hath lain away.

No cumbrous bars of the oaken wood,
   No walls of the granite stone,
Needeth he now to preserve that good
   Which once was his care alone.

He soundly sleeps in his midnight bed,
   Nor feareth he for his pelf;
No loaded pistols are 'neath his head,
   No daggers near on the shelf.

He trembles no more at the watchman's tread,
   As he paceth his nightly round;
And he quakes not with that olden dread
   At the least mysterious sound.

But a shrewd old fellow he grows each day,
   And has found, to his heart's content,
That better than packing of dollars away
   Is the grateful cent per cent.

SOLDIER, COME HOME!

Addressed particularly to Captain John H. Jackson, of Portsmouth, N. H., engaged in the war with Mexico.

Soldier, come home! There waits a heart-felt greeting
Thy coming by thy own hearth-stone again;
The gladdest smiles will bless the happy meeting,
And tears bedew thy neck like summer rain, —
Shed from bright eyes that wept at thy departing,
For the stern destiny that bid thee roam, —
But joy will prompt the tears that then are starting.
Soldier, come home!

Soldier, come home! The weary, weary hours
Have left their marks on those thou left behind!
There 's many a thorn grown rankling 'mid the flowers,
There 's many a gray lock with the dark entwined;
The heart alone unchanged, thy form has guarded,
Prayed for thy weal 'mid battle's dire alarms,
Hoped for the time when fear should be discarded
Within thine arms.

SILVER vs. TIN;

OR, CHILDHOOD IN ITS CUPS.

I SAW a rich man's child, with gloomy air,
  Holding a silver cup within her hand,
The cup well filled with some rich beverage rare,
  Mixed by a maid who by her side did stand;
With petulance she raised the honeyed drink,
  And, quicker than the eye the thought could trace,
Ere the meek maiden had a chance to wink,
  Dash went the sweetening in her patient face!
I thought within myself that, should it come,
And I 'd a child like that, I 'd give it "some."

I saw a poor man's child, with cup of tin,
  Sitting and singing by her father's door;
Treacle and water were the cup within, —
  Treacle quite tart, the water dreadful poor;
And as the child trilled forth a cheerful note, —
  ("O, don't you cry, Susannah," was the tune), —
Anon she moistenéd her little throat
  By small libations from an iron spoon;
And here methought that silver could not buy
The happiness that glistened in her eye.

Soldier, come home! Ah, how the full heart, yearning,
Has wildly throbbed to measures of thy fame;
Affection's eye still to the glad line turning
That bore due tribute to thy gallant name;
With quick pulse beating at each passing story,
Telling of valiant deeds on many a field,
Till, catching fire from the tale of glory,
All fears did yield!

Soldier, come home! From strange airs danger breathing,
To scenes remembered by the camp-fire's blaze,
When Fancy fond her images was wreathing,
And home and friends were present to thy gaze;
The star-lit picture of thy midnight dreaming
Return and verify, no more to roam,
And scenes, delights, with which thy mind was teeming,
Enjoy at home.

Soldier, come home! Bring back the faithful token
That interposed thy precious life to save, —*
A sister's love-charm, like a chain unbroken,
Releasing not its spell this side the grave, —
And wear it as a God-gift when in haven,
As when around thee strife's wild waves did rage,
And on thy heart may its high truths be graven,
A brilliant page!

* He had a little Testament, a gift from a sister, in his breast-pocket.

Soldier, come home! From War's rude shocks recover;
  Cast by the sword for implement of peace;
May her bright spirit o'er thy pathway hover,
  And bid thy weary soul its troubles cease;
The guerdon of a grateful country's praise
  Shall be a halo round thy passing years,
And the bold story of thy battle days
                Glad greedy ears.

THE UNION.

Heaven save our glorious Union, and save it in its might,
With ne'er a wind to blow it harm, and ne'er a frost to
blight;
Most stanchly has it stood by us in happiness and woe,
And we 'll cling to it for safety as our chiefest hope below.

'T is twined in power around our land — an adamantine
chain,
Forged long ago, in blood and strife, on many a battle-
plain —
Forged, too, by northern men and south, with earnest
thoughts impressed,
Who held this thought the holiest that burned within
their breast.

The iron of their earnest souls was welded in its strength,
And faith and hope, that knew no bound, were measured
in its length;

They wound it round each hearth and home, a hallowed thing and blest,
A sacred ark to cherish true, a shield when trouble pressed.

When war-clouds broke upon our land, within its circling might
A power strong was found to put all hostile ills to flight,
And warmest blessings crowned the bond that rendered safety sure,
And vows arose to love it long, from grateful hearts and pure;

To teach it to the rising age, a watch-word for its day,
When its framers and their counsels should have passed from earth away;
To be a light upon the wave, a beacon on the shore,
In whose serene unfailing ray were safety evermore.

The Union!—'t is a tower of strength that puny arms may threat;
Its basis is the people's heart, and is not shaken yet;
The teeth that strive to gnaw the chain shall find its metal true,
Its strength a world of power yet not easy to subdue.

O! palsied be the hand to give the sacrilegious blow,
To lay this temple of our hopes in desolation low,
To dash to earth the altar-fires that blaze within the fane,
The blood of Freedom's sacrifice thus offered up in vain!

But we 'll cling to it — we 'll cling to it — and the people
in their might
Shall once again re-ratify the charter of their right;
For the Union they have spoken, in tones that may not
swerve,
And vow in solemn majesty the UNION TO PRESERVE!

NOTE. — The above was sent to Ensign Stebbings, for his approval. It found the ensign just as he had concluded his Fourth of July dinner, at which unusually good appetite had prevailed, and the sentiments of the season had been remarkably spirited and patriotic, in view of recent events. He read the poem attentively, his eye beamed with unwonted fire, he grasped instinctively the carving-knife! — but, at that moment, he was recalled to a state of calmness by some one asking him for a piece of the pig; and, putting the poem carefully in his pocket-book, he placed it in the side-pocket next his patriotic heart. He was too full to speak.

A PLEASURE TRIP TO HAMPTON.

A "POEM," OF COURSE.

THE day is warm, and very muggy,
And Mr. Sled he has a notion
That he will take the horse and buggy,
And Mrs. Sled, to see the ocean.

And Mrs. Sled has coaxed her Mister,
And he, the dear kind-hearted man,
Has given consent to take her sister, —
A slight departure from his plan.

Then Johnny and Mally,
And Bobby and Sally,
And little Joe Alley, less stocking or shoe,
Set up such a clatter,
That, to settle the matter,
The kind Mr. Sled says they may go too.

And then he lays in lots of pickings,
Mammoth dough-nuts, legs of chickens,

Apple-pies and ginger-bread, —
A bounteous man is Mr. Sled, —
For prices down at Hampton Beach
Are very far beyond his reach.

Then he takes a small bottle and fills it, the while
Mrs. Sled and her sister agreeably smile,
And all is packed snug, and away o'er the road
The horse, like a cynic, *making light* of his load.

O, Hampton Beach! no power of speech
Can half thy wondrous beauties teach!
Where the cool air brings on its lively wings
A generous zest for the victuals and things!
Where you wash in the spray, — or rather you *may*,
Should your inclination " cotton " that way.
(But don't do like him who decency shocks,
Undress openly down on the rocks,
Exposed to the gaze of the passers-by,
Who may look that way with a careless eye;
But go into the houses, and put on thin "trouses,"
And then you can bathe with sweet hearts or spouses,
Indulging in multitudinous souses.)
Where the force of the spray knocks you every way,
And chance is afforded to pretty things say,
And to show off brave, as you daringly lave
In the rushing whirl of the incoming wave!

Arrived at the spot, out Mr. Sled got,
And took out the lot as quick as a shot,

And down on the grass the eatables " *sot.*"
The old horse, tied to the limb of a tree,
Thought to himself, " What nincoms are we,
To come so far,
With jolt and jar,
Just for to go for to see the sea ! "
The horse did n't think in very good grammar,
But he could n't, — the breakers made such a clamor.

Now Mr. Sled placidly paces the sand,
With his spouse and her sister on either hand;
While the urchins, stockingless, bare to the knees,
Are revelling high in those " Tails of the Seas,"
Where the big waves come, with a rush and roar,
And expend themselves on the trembling shore,
Then rushing and roaring back again,
As if to play with the children they 'd fain,
The little ones clapping their hands in fun,
As after them down the sands they run.

" Now really, my dear," says Mr. Sled,
" If 't were n't for this 'ere cold in my head,
I 'd be out there in the wink of an eye,
The force of them furious waves to try, —
I can't stand still, I 'm tempted so,
I 'm almost persuaded, — I vow I *will* go."

This was a clincher; and Mrs. Sled,
Like a sensible woman, ne'er opened her head;

He knew what was best,
And as for the rest,
They neither opinion nor warning expressed,
So up to the buggy he went and undressed;
Or he changed his garb to a suitable suit, —
'T was a mystery how he managed to do 't, —
But he cast his slough, and from heel to head
A comical chicken was Mr. Sled!

Stockingless, hatless, with shirt of check,
Tied snugly with tape around his neck,
Pantaloons blue, with a patch on each knee,
And fitting as tight as the skin could be.
Then the ladies blushed, and a laugh did smother,
But the sister blushed much more than the other.
To tell the truth, 't was a curious fix
To be seen by a virgin of forty-six!

Then darted he boldly the beach along,
Then dashed he wildly the waves among,
Then stood upright,
That a wave in sight
Might fall upon him in all its might!
And the ladies uttered a thrilling screech,
To see Mr. S. roll over the beach,
Like — I don't know what to compare him to —
Perhaps a dolphin, but rather more blue.
But he soon appeared, with a smile most bland,
His clothes and his hair well covered with sand,

And expressed, in words that were not so plain,
The thoughts that he should try it again.

Then the ladies — Heaven bless them! —
Said *they'd* go and *dress* them,
And see how the waves in their sport would caress them,
If Mr. Sled, the best of old fellows,
Would promise his wife he would n't be jealous.

Now two such brides,
For the living tides,
No one saw, Mr. Sled besides,
You wonder, perhaps, how *I* got hold of it —
I only know it, as Mr. Sled told of it.

I always thought the dresses were shorter
The ladies had to wear into the water,
But theirs were as long and as black as soot,
And below the feet about a foot.
They tied a white cap 'neath the chin,
With every sprig of a curl tucked in, —
From the description, I should agree it
Would be most delectable fun to see it, —
And such a trio the world ne'er knew
As Mr. Sled and the other two!
Then down all three
Went into the sea,
Laughing with most ineffable glee.
Rolling and roaring the big wave came,

Angry and high did it rear its head,
An instant only, and lo! the dame
And the spinster both were hurled in shame,
And piled on top of Mr. Sled!

I forgot to say the sky grew dark,
A fact which they had n't seemed to mark,
And the first thing that made her look on high
Was when Mrs. Sled got a drop in her eye.
"I declare it rains — we shall get wet through!
Mr. Sled, what upon airth shall we do?"
"Why, fretting, my dear, won't better make it —
I think we 'd better stand and take it."
So their garments they change as best they may,
Each one looking the "other way,"
And then, to avoid the rainy weather,
They all crawl under the buggy together,
And pass round among them the eatables nice,
That are greedily snatched and ate in a trice.
Then Mr. Sled takes from some secret place,
And holds up to view, with a smiling face,
That little bottle I spoke of before, —
Holding a half a pint or more, —
And with a nod round, a health to denote,
He pours a small portion adown his own throat,
Then smacking his lips, his joy to express,
He passes the liquid the others to bless;
They take it, and nod back, and smilingly look,
But they thought the spinster the largest share took;
I don't say it was so, — care nothing about it, —
The story would go on quite well without it.

Now it rained and rained, as it never would done,
Till it leaked through the buggy, and down on them run;
Again Mrs. Sled asked what they *should* do,
And the children and spinster looked dismally blue;
But Mr. S.
Smiled never the less,
Nor gave a sign denoting distress;
Indifferent he to the falling tide,
As the horse who, " smoking," stood outside.

Their patience worn out, they gained their taps,
And gathered for home their scattered traps;
But ere they started did Mr. S.
These lines of reason and rhyme express,
Sealed with a doughnut, and nailed to a tree,
That wanderers there might the lesson see:
" *A rainy day at Hampton Beach*
Will test all the rules philosophers teach."

MORAL.

I trust that this story the moral will teach, —
Just reckon the cost when you go to the beach,
And see if your pockets contain the tin,
If it rains, to admit you the hotel within.
Be sure that you have it, I tell you, because
To be there without it you 're a cat without claws;
Besides, 't is to show that a true man will bear
What would drive many others to utter despair,
And look at this truth-telling ditty you 've read,
And practise the virtues of rare Mr. Sled.

TO THE OLD INKSTAND,

ON RECEIVING A PRESENT OF A NEW ONE.

LONG hast thou stood by me, old friend,
But our companionship must end,
For Tompkins doth another send,
My praise to wake;
You must depart, and I intend
New stand to take.

Full many an hour has seen me skim
For ideas round thy dingy brim,
And sometimes, answering to my whim,
I 've drawn them out,
As anglers draw from recess dim
The speckled trout.

I bless thee for the good thou 'st done,
I 've found within thy depths some fun,
A joke or so — some feeble one —
Have brought to view;
But now good-bye, — thy ink has run, —
I 'll try the new.

Depart, old cup, your rest to take,
And no expostulation make,
My new resolve you cannot shake,
You 're on the shelf;
But nothing can my friendship break,
Old thing of delf.

SATURDAY NIGHT;

OR, A SOMEWHAT WORLDLY VIEW OF A RATHER SERIOUS TIME, WHERE THE SOLACES OF EARTH ARE SUPPOSED TO CROWD DOWN MORE SPIRITUAL INFLUENCES.

Well, Saturday has come again—
The night of all the nights is here;
Regarded world-wide as the pause
In labor's wearisome career.

The pleasing sound of hard-earned cash
Has lulled the soul to tranquil rest;
The "ready" has a potent charm
To ease the troubles of the breast.

Virtue has not like this the power
To soothe the heart oppressed by woe;
Experience tells us every hour
She rarely bides with men below.

Her influence, reckoned as the balm
To cool the fever of earth's ills,
Can never boast the healing charm
That rests in good and current bills.

Their rustling, like the sound of leaves,
  In the bright, bland summer night,
The eager, care-worn soul receives,
  Rejoicing in a new delight.

O, how the days in turmoil pass, —
  A thousand pressing trials vex us, —
Until we long, in vain, alas!
  To flee the land, and go to — Texas, —

To throw the weary body by,
  Or cast the bitter care that fills us;
When, like an answer to our prayer,
  Comes Saturday along, and stills us.

But many are the means and ways
  This resting season for enjoying;
Some lose themselves in pleasure's maze,
  And some the hour are worse employing.

Some drug their souls in Cyprian bowers,
  Lured on to death by venal charms,
And cast their fortunes and their powers
  To the false trust of treacherous arms.

Happy the man who finds his *home*,
  The rightful spot to spend the season;
Whose passions, checked, nor left to roam,
  Are made subservient to reason.

Who heedeth not the proud man's sneer,
  Or that a callous world may flout him;
Well pleased his children's breath to hear,
  Harmonious in their sleep about him.

No horrors rack his sleeping head,
  Based on hot suppers, pipes, or steaming;
But radiant angels round his bed
  Infuse bright fancies in his dreaming.

Blest goal! to which the toiling heart
  Can look as for its solace given,
And claim thee, as indeed thou art,
  The happiest night of all the seven!

THE LITTLE GRAVE REVISITED.

FRIENDSHIP seeks the little grave ;
Spring's gay glories o'er it wave,
Sunshine rests upon the scene,
Freshly bright, the grass is green.

Here summer clouds their drops may shed,
Like tears, above this lowly bed;
And zephyrs whisper notes of woe
For the loved one who sleeps below.

Here flowers may their fragrance pour,
Meet offering for a holy hour,
And songs of birds, in cadence clear,
Seem angel tones our hearts to cheer.

Friendship seeks the little grave,
Autumn's tokens o'er it wave,
Nature's richest hues are seen,
Brightly mingled gold and green.

No tablet marks the sacred spot
Our pilgrim steps have hereward brought;
The turfy hillock only shows
Where she, the loved, doth still repose.

We sighing muse upon the past,
On joys too pure and high to last,
And grief, that fell with chilling blight
When her bright sun went down in night; —

Faded, as fades the glow of day,
Passed, as pass spring flowers away, —
From earth's corruption heavenward fled,
More blest than we who mourned her dead.

Friendship seeks the little grave,
Leafless branches o'er it wave, —
Winter's snow usurps the scene,
No more now the grass is green.

Returning spring-time shall restore
Its genial garniture once more;
Again shall brightest verdure wave
Above the little silent grave.

Unlike the season's changeful hue,
Our memory shall be always true;
Forever there shall fondly dwell
Her image that we loved so well.

Still we 'll seek the little grave,
From which affection could not save,
And grasp the hope that sundered love
Shall reünited be above.

A SLEIGHING SONG.

Over the snow, over the snow,
Away we go, away we go!
    The earth gleams white
    'Neath the stars to-night,
    And all is bright
        Above and below.

Old Care, good-by! old Care, good-by!
From you we fly, from you we fly, —
    As if on wings,
    Our fleet steed springs,
    And the welkin rings
        With our joyous cry.

Gay Mirth is here, gay Mirth is here,
Our hearts to cheer, our hearts to cheer;
    While on we glide,
    There 's one by our side,
    To cheer or to chide,
        Who is always dear.

Over the snow, over the snow,
Away we go, away we go!
    There 's freedom rare
    Abroad in the air,
    Everywhere,
        Above and below.

THE FEARFUL OATH;

OR, SOME ACCOUNT OF THE WICKED MR. JONES.

O, A wicked man was 'Bimelech Jones,
  A wickeder one was rare, was rare;
At lying and fibbing "he made no bones,"
  And awfully bad he'd swear, he'd swear.

His voice was harsh as a north-west gale,
  And hoarse and loud was his laugh, his laugh,
Libations oft, in the foaming ale,
  To slake his thirst, he'd quaff, he'd quaff.

His step was a bold and sturdy tread,
  That seemed to jar where it prest, it prest;
And those familiar, who heard it, said
  They knew it o'er all the rest, the rest.

Now, rich grew 'Bimelech Jones apace,
  Which softened his sins most strange, most strange;
Smiles greeted him from every face,
  And his word was law upon 'change, on change.

And a haughty man was 'Bimelech Jones,
He bowed not to God or man, or man;
And once he swore, by his blood and bones, —
'T was thus his strange oath ran, it ran: —

That Death over him should ne'er prevail,
However hard he might try, might try;
From whatever quarter he chose to assail,
He, 'Bimelech Jones, would n't die, would n't die.

O, how the flesh crept of those who heard!
The blood in their veins ran cold, ran cold;
But spoken and writ was the awful word,
From the lips of the bad man bold, so bold!

Now, time flew by, and the fleet years shed
Upon 'Bimelech Jones their mark, their mark;
The snows of age rested upon his head,
And his vision grew dim and dark, and dark.

But still did he vow he would not die,
And laughed at counsel for good, for good;
He looked on high at the bright blue sky,
And scoffed at it there as he stood, as he stood.

But missed was he when the summer sun
In the heavens above rode high, rode high;
And missed was he when the day was done,
And night in its gloom drew nigh, drew nigh.

And people marvelled that he came not,
  As was his wont, to mart, to mart;
That he should forsake that favorite spot,
  Where to cash he 'd coined his heart, his heart.

They sought him at home in his chamber drear,
  And they opened its door with dread, with dread;
And their hearts quaked then with an awful fear,
  As they stood face to face with the dead, the dead.

Sate 'Bimelech Jones in his old arm-chair,
  Death's seal on his brow was set, was set;
His open eyes glared with a stony stare,
  As if life were biding there yet, there yet.

But death had triumphed, — the vow was broke, —
  Old 'Bimelech Jones was dead, was dead;
But he fell not like others beneath the stroke,
  For he died with his hat on his head, on his head.

Sitting there his table-side by,
  Like life, his papers among, among;
But the fire had all gone out from his eye,
  And silent and cold was his tongue, his tongue.

Then Coroner Smith some hard dollars took,
  And jingled them well in his ear, his ear;
But he started not, though loudly they shook,
  Which, living, he 'd jump to hear, to hear.

They knew that the spirit had left the clay,
  Not to wake at that musical chink, that chink;
His ear, so alive to its sound alway,
  No longer its music would drink, would drink!

Now, each night 't is said that 'Bimelech Jones
  Revisits the scene where he died, he died,
And with his loud knockings and piteous groans
  The people are sore terrified, terrified.

THE FIRST ROBIN OF SPRING.

I AM Robin the First of the kingdom of song,
  And my throne is the bough of the old cherry-tree;
The zephyrs of spring bear my mandates along,
  And the gentle and good are all subject to me.

Glad, glad is the home near whose precincts I stay,
  A grant to abide I repay with delight;
My matin shall cheer it at dawn of the day,
  And my vesper hymn bless it at coming of night.

As when in the gay bowers of Eden 't was sung,
  I sing to the world my melodious strain;
And the heart that is sad the earth's discords among
  May turn, with my notes, back to Eden again.

I am Robin the First of the kingdom of song,
  My sceptre the power of melody sweet;
The summer's glad months my rule shall prolong,
  And its flowery trophies be laid at my feet.

"DANIEL WEBSTER IS NO MORE!"

'T WAS Sabbath morning, still and clear,
  And fair uprose the ruddy sun,
When burst upon our startled ear
  The booming of the mournful gun.

The sound of fear smote every breast,
  As, echoing round from hill to shore,
It broke the peaceful Sabbath-rest,
  Proclaiming Webster was no more!

No more! and has that mighty mind
  Sunk to the sleep that knows no dreams?
Has that effulgent sun declined,
  That rayed our country with its beams?

No more! and shall that glowing tongue,
  Which thrilled the people by its tone,
When through their heart of hearts it rung,
  Be left to dark decay alone?

And must that glance of living light,
  Whose meteor brightness waked our fear,
Fade, all obscured, in deepest night,
  And leave us, dazzled, groping here?

No more! Not so, — on history's page,
  Inscribed in characters of flame,
A mark for every coming age,
  Is seen the glory of his name.

His acts shall live, his voice be heard,
  In mightier cadence than of old;
Its eloquence embalms each word,
  E'en though his tongue in death be cold.

The mighty soul has riven the clay
  That bound it with encumbering chains;
The earthly form may know decay,
  The heavenly principle remains,

To guide the patriot heart aright,
  When waves of harsh discordance rise,
To be a beacon ever bright
  When angry clouds enshroud our skies.

Then say not "Webster is no more;" —
  That from our counsels he has fled; —
More living still* than e'er before,
  Is he — the mighty — mourned as dead!

* "I STILL LIVE!"

A RETROSPECTION.

A panoramic scope of years
  Is seen through retrospection's glass,
And showers of tributary tears
  Confirm the pictures as they pass.

Pass ye, the joys of early hours;
  Pass ye, the friends of other days;
Pass all, who strewed my path with flowers
  That bloomed in youth's primeval rays!

Return, the distant and the dead,
  The voices of the fruitful past,
The buoyant mind long, long since fled,
  The hopes too bright and fair to last!

I see again a gladsome hearth,
  An echo hear of distant glee;
Bright eyes still beam with love and mirth,
  And turn their fondest gaze on me!

Stay, vision bright! my fainting soul
  Would leave the misty future's track,
And to that blessed starting-goal
  Would look for hope and solace back.

Alas! 't is fading as I gaze, —
The pictures have in beauty flown, —
And left, for memory of those days,
The stern reality of our own.

The dust of many mouldering years
Obscures the blessed vision sped,
And the libation of our tears
Is now on memory's altar shed.

RUBBISH ABOUT AN OLD HOUSE.

THE moments of the old house now are numbered,
Pull it away;
The space is wanted it so long hath cumbered,
For use to-day.

Now thundering fall each olden beam and rafter,
Pull them away;
They fall amid the shouting and the laughter
Of men to-day.

Now fall its sides — the inner view revealing
Old Time's decay;
The crumbling plaster and worm-eaten ceiling
Dropping away!

But, as we gaze, can fancy not awaken
Some old dream sped,
Peopling these rooms, lone, dreary and forsaken,
With forms long fled?

Pass now before us faces beauty beaming, —
Childhood and youth, —
Scenes are enacted in our noon-day dreaming,
Vivid as truth.

Alternate changes mark the just presentment,
Like to a life;
Fiery Ambition, Hatred, Love, Contentment,
Hope, Peace and Strife;

All are portrayed, — the funeral and the bridal, —
From woe to joy;
Fancy still plies her wand, and, never idle,
Yet finds employ.

Age after age sweeps by in quick succession,
And, as we scan,
The history tell throughout the long procession;
The doom of man.

And as moves by each fleeting generation, —
Whate'er his fame, —
Is read the truth that man in every station
Is still the same.

As the old house falleth when its place is needed,
So falleth man,
Like an old ruin by the world unheeded —
'T is nature's plan.

A grander fabric springs upon his ruin,
Raised from the clod,
Taking eternal durance with renewing, —
The builder GOD.

RUM REMINISCENCES;

OR, THE OLD TOPER WAXING PATHETIC.

Let us speak of times that were, Jim,
  Of hours that used to pass,
Noted by other glasses, Jim,
  Besides the hour-glass;
Brim full were they with pleasure, Jim,
  Bright joy shone in our cup,
And greedy we for bliss, Jim,
  Soon drank the jewel up.

O, well do we remember, Jim,
  The bottles in a row,
The lemons dotted in between, —
  A fascinating show;
The counters filled with glasses, Jim,
  Decanters marshalled bold,
With the cocktails and the juleps,
  And the punches hot and cold.

How the diamond drop of mirth, Jim,
  Stood beaming on the lip,
And how the fun would sparkle, Jim,
  As we 'd the nectar sip!

The songs we gayly sung, Jim,
  The stories that we told,
Have lost the charm they used to have,
  Now we are growing old.

With blinded eyes we strayed, Jim,
  Nor dreamt of danger nigh, —
That every draught concealed a shaft,
  And each cup nursed a sigh;
That halcyon moments fleeing, Jim,
  To us, then young and brave,
Were naught but subtle quicksands, Jim,
  Where we might find a grave.

A thrill comes o'er the sailor, Jim,
  When morning brings to light
Some danger dread just passed, Jim,
  Concealed within the night;
And can we never feel, Jim,
  In view of dangers past,
A gratitude that we were spared
  Destruction's sweeping blast?

The time to come looks bright, Jim,
  No cloud obscures the day;
The evil spirits, once our bane,
  We 've banished far away!
The chain is broke, — we 're free, Jim,
  From bonds that bound us sore,
And joy we feel we never felt
  In old rum days of yore.

THE MINER'S RETURN.

Ah, who shall tell of the miner's thought,
  As his native land rises before him,
Her mountains in mist of the distance wrought,
  And her atmosphere floating o'er him!

He has toiled in hope of a glad return
  To bless whom his parting gave sorrow;
And his soul with enkindled hope doth yearn,
  As he thinks on the near to-morrow.

The night settles down on the ocean wide,
  And the light-house fire is beaming,
And wild as the ocean and swift as its tide
  Are the dreams the miner is dreaming.

Fond fancy bringeth a bright array
  Of joyful faces near him,
A father's blessing, and the gladdening play
  Of a mother's smile, to cheer him;

A wife's embrace, and the smile and tear
  That speak a blissful sadness,
And the gleesome shout of children dear,
  In childhood's boisterous gladness.

And the welcome grasp of friendly hands,
  And friendly voices, greet him;
Each well-known tree by the way-side stands,
  Like an old friend out to meet him.

No adverse cloud broods o'er the scene,
  With ills portent to lower,
But a bow of hope spans the sky serene,
  As might follow a golden shower.

And golden towers in golden light
  Shine rich in golden glory,
And golden spires like fingers write
  In gold the golden story.

And golden founts, with ceaseless play,
  Surpass that fountain olden,
Whose waters broke in golden spray
  On sands whose grains were golden.

And golden bright are the leaves of the trees,
  That with golden blossoms mingle,
And the song of the birds and hum of the bees
  Have a sort of golden jingle.

And he laughed aloud in his gorgeous dream,
  Unmarred by doubt or sorrow,
And far away to his waking did seem
  That near approaching morrow.

It dawns, and 'neath the golden sun
  Shine rock, and tree, and tower;
The long-wished goal is nearly won,
  His home he will see in an hour.

And then perchance will his ardent hope
  Come lost in a blest fruition,
And as bright a day of promise ope
  As e'er graced his sleeping vision.

But sad was the story that met his ear:
  His parents by death were stricken,
And his children in damps of poverty drear
  Like blighted plants did sicken;

And their hollow eyes glared on his anguished face,
  As they told the tale how their mother
Had left them long the heirs of disgrace,
  And fled away with another.

Then the golden dream was all dispelled,
  And he bowed his head in sorrow,
And wished that an ocean grave had withheld
  That much yearned for to-morrow.

CITY PHILOSOPHY; OR, BEES AND BIRDS vs. BUGS.

How to make one's self happy by adopting the principle of Sir Reynard, of sour-grape memory, in anticipation of the time when pecuniary obstruction shall debar the humble from rural delights.

Poets may tell us of flower-clad bowers
And shady groves and halcyon hours;
Of quiet nooks
And babbling brooks,
And simple fish to be caught with hooks;
Of dreams beneath some wide-spread tree,
By streams that loiteringly seek the sea,
Hugging their banks with gurgling song,
And kissing each as they move along,—
They may say
You can stay
The live-long day
(That is, if you have a turn that way),
Beside some little fresh-water bay,
And see o'er its surface the dragon-fly play,
And list to the mill sounding far away,
Or the farmer-boys singing while making hay,
Or the bees as they rifle the flowers gay,
Or the birds on the spray,
As they tune their lay,
Shaded by trees from the warm sun's ray;

They may by their story
  Make each nymph of the dairy
A being all glory,
  An angel or fairy;
With eyes brightly shining
  As rare diamonds glow,
With curls gayly twining
  O'er neck white as snow;
With grace in her form,
  And health in her cheek;
With heart beating warm,
  Each act doth bespeak;
A creature all heaven,
  With no taint of sin,
A thing to earth given,
  'T were heaven to win;
They may sing, if they please,
Of the teeming trees,
Yielding their fruits to the farmer's will,
Of the sports of the field,
Which rare fun yield,
Where the cracking gun is heard "to kill."
They may sum up the joys of a country life,
They may rail at the city 's noise and strife,
Or scenes of the town with trouble rife;

BUT:

There are odious bugs in airy bowers,
They dwell in the trees and dwell in the flowers;
There are bugs in the earth, there are bugs in the air,
There are bugs in the water and everywhere;

You may throw yourself on the ground along,
To list to the fife-bird's glorious song;
You may hear it and dream, and dream as you hear,
And wake up, at last, with a bug in your ear;
You may roam, if you will, by the crystal brook,
To tempt the fish with deceiving hook,
You may drag your line from morn till night,
And be oftener getting bit than a bite;
You may plunge in depths of the forest shade,
You may mount the hill or roam the glade,
In bush or in brake, in dingle or dell,
There are bugs, there are bugs, more than pen can tell;
And the rural Venus warmly portrayed,
   In colors drawn from the poet's heart,
May prove, at best, but some country maid
   Driving her father's market-cart,
With cheeks burnt red by a summer sun,
   With coarse brown hair and freckled brow,
Whose stalwart arm might a furrow run
   The live-long day behind the plough.
But were it not so, — were every grace
   As vivid as he describes in his fair, —
'T is something peculiar to no clime or place,
   But woman's own attribute everywhere.

Through the forest and over the hill
   You drag your gun from morn till night,
Sometimes seeing a bird to kill
   That is less in danger from shot than fright;

Wading the brook and washed to the knees,
  Laden with multitudinous freight;
Your game-bag plenished with bread and cheese,
  Mingling in with worms for bait!
There 's an invite comes from the cooling west,
That calls to you 'neath the trees to rest;
You bare your brow to the genial air,
And inhale the perfumes wafted there,
    You dream not of woe,
    There 's a heavenly glow
    Cast all over the world below;
When a humming is heard, and with terrible din
Mosquitos their afternoon meal begin,
And the way they pick at you is a sin!
Punching your body with myriad holes,—
In vain is your cry, " Get out, *bless* your souls!"
    They heed no more
    Your cries so sore
    Than they would if a sucking lamb should roar!
You mark just now the waning sun,
And shoulder again your trusty gun;
Bit upon face and bit upon neck,
What can your homeward speed now check?
You traverse a mile, and recall to mind
You have left your game-bag far behind;
Then back you plod with a weary pace,
Perhaps like a school-boy "lose the place,"
Finding the bag beneath the trees,
But the black ants eating your bread and cheese.

* * * * * *

Homeward bound! homeward bound!
Earnestly hoped and blessed when found.
Give me the city, — the noisy mart, —
The cry of the man with the charcoal-cart;
The oysterman's note when night is still,
More plaintive than song of whippoorwill;
Sleeping at morn as my pleasure incline;
Dining at two, as a Christian should dine;
Sitting up an hour or so after tea, —
        Give me these, if you please,
And a country life go to others for me.

THE ANTIQUATED CHAPEAU.

I remember — I remember —
 That Hat, now worn and dim,
When glossy shone its silky crown,
 And eke its curling rim;
When Sundays donned it glory shed
 Upon the suit below,
The glancing sunshine in its sheen
 Received an added glow.

I remember — I remember —
 When to the house 't was brought,
The wily jokes that passed around
 In asking who was *caught;*
The repartee that darted back;
 The answer prompt and pat;
The full receipt — stop — was it so?
 I can't remember *that.*

I remember — I remember —
 When first it 'gan to fade,
To save it from a fast decay
 The efforts that were made;

The ink put on the browning spots,
And ironed once a week ; —
But fading beauty spoke more plain
Than tongue could ever speak.

I remember — I remember —
When last that hat was worn,
Its top was rusty at the verge,
Its rim was sadly torn ;
Its polished sheen had vanished all
That charmed in other days —
Its crown a continent of felt,
Indented round with bays.

I remember — I remember —
What parsons used to say,
When I attended to their calls,
That all things must decay ;
Then let me wisdom gain from thee,
My old hat on the shelf,
And heed the lesson thou dost teach, —
I must decay myself.

OLD TIMES.

TO JOHN T. CHESLEY, ESQ., OF LOWELL.

I DARE say you remember, John,
Back twenty years and more,
When we were young and jolly, John,
On old Cocheco's shore ;
When our paths were bright and fair, John,
And the hours most deftly sped,
With our hearts as free from care, John,
As the breezes round our head.

And don't you sometimes see, John,
Full many a scene and face,
That memory, true to life, John,
Restores with pristine grace ;
The smiles of old companions, John,
The music of their voice,
That through the damps of many years
Yet make your heart rejoice ?

Dost ever roam in fancy, John,
Amid those dark old woods ?
Dost ever lave in wantonness,
Within Cocheco's floods ?

Dost hear the booming dam, John,
  At evening, calm and still,
Or the dashing of the busy wheel
  That turns the droning mill?

Dost remember Log-Hill spring, John,
  Whose waters were so sweet,
That poured its treasures lovingly
  In crystal at our feet,
While the birds sang in the pines, John,
  A sweet and mellow strain,
That older ears in after years
  May never hear again?

Ah, halcyon days were those, John,
  Our lines how golden bright!
With not an ill to vex us, John,
  And not a care to fright,
We laughed the hours away, John,
  In unconcern of fate,
Nor saw how near the Boy's domain
  Bordered on Man's estate.

I turn my eyes oft back, John,
  And busy memory true,
In answer to my call, John,
  Brings old scenes to my view;
I see myself among them, John,
  So young and blithe and free,
Then view myself as time has made, —
  I'm quite another me.

I meet with old-time friends, John,
  With whom we daily met,
Whose smiles endeared the passing hours,
  But me they now forget;
They are gray and weary men, John,
  Their cheerfulness all spent,
And, worldly given, grope through life,
  In adding cent to cent.

But there are true ones too, John,
  That stick through weal and woe,
Whose friendship waits not fortune's breeze
  A favoring gale to blow,
Whose generous hearts are ready, John,
  To hold us in embrace,
Our names enrolled in letters there
  That Time may not efface.

Alas! the changing world, John;
  Old scenes make way for new;
The builder's hand has closed our paths,
  Or railroads run them through;
But let us thank our stars, John,
  That active Fancy teems,
And what time's rubber may destroy
  We may restore in dreams.

A RHYME ABOUT A BABY.

One Saturday night
(I forget me quite
Whether 't was stormy, or whether 't was bright),
As Mr. Haiz and his good wife sat,
Somewhat later than was their way,
Talking o'er about this and that
Of what had happened throughout the day, —
A little domestic council of two,
Discussing as gravely as cabinets do,
Laying out plans for coming days; —
For a prudent man was Solomon Haiz,
And his wife, Mrs. Haiz, search the town all around,
A prudenter woman could n't be found.

They had just arrived at the dreamy state,
And for bed were about to adjourn debate,
For the hour was getting rather late,
When the door-bell rang
With a terrible clang,
And upon their taps the Haizes sprang.

Now, a bolder man than Solomon Haiz
Cannot be found in these latter days,

But he trembled at the din;
He turned the matter in his mind
Of what or whom he there should find,
And whether to let them in.

Then he seized the lamp — to the door he went —
"Who 's there?" thrice shouted, with all his might;
No answer returned — his patience was spent —
He opened the door, and looked out on the night;
Boldly outward he thrust the light,
But there was n't a moving thing in sight;
The lamp's bright glare,
In the midnight air,
Cast horrible shadows here and there,
And worse shape he 'd never seen before
Than his own, revealed on his half-closed door.

He lookéd out and lookéd around,
And up and down with eager eye,
When glimmering white below, on the ground,
At his out-thrust foot did a basket lie.

*   *   *   *   *   *   *

The door slammed to with a terrible din,
Waking the house with dire alarms,
When Mr. Haiz, to his wife's amaze,
Walked straight in with a babe in his arms!

Now a scene occurred, as a player might say,
'T would require an able pen to portray,
For things did look in a serious way;

For Mrs. Haiz,
With her face in a blaze,
Seemed struck mute with a fit of amaze;
While poor Mr. Haiz
Looked forty ways,
Unable to meet her fiery gaze.

But 't was none of his, he vowed by his gods,
And why it was left there he could n't tell;
The dame replied by incredulous nods,
And a look whose meaning he knew full well.

Then zealously opened a new debate,
And long to agree they were quite unable;
He could n't hold out, for the subject's weight
Made Mr. Haiz move it might lie on the table.

Then they unpinned the wrapper to look at the child,
And, as for conquest, the little elf
Looked up at the lady and sweetly smiled,
Till she grew good-natured in spite of herself.

Now, a chick nor child the Haizes had not,
Although they had room and plenty of tin;
And anger gave way to a gentler thought,
And they took the young night-coming stranger in.

The next day being Sunday, to church they went,
And the babe was christened Abijah Haiz,
And the little waif thus heaven sent
Was a comfort to them all their days.

Whether right or not right,
On that Saturday night,
To leave the baby where he might spy him,
Every one says
That Solomon Haiz
Acted *just like a father* by him.

THE BAR-KEEPER'S DREAM.

'T WAS midnight in the bar-room dim,
The revellers had flown,
The bar-man looked around with fear
To find himself alone;
An icy chill lay at his heart
He ne'er before had known.

He stood within his silent bar,
He felt the dismal gloom!
The lamps' dull glare cast here and there
Dim shadows round the room;
His spirit felt a sense as sad
As if 't were in a tomb.

And thought, which in the hour of glee
He never would allow,
And conscience, with its awful voice,
Long hushed, he well knew how,
Both came upon him in that hour,
And busy were they now.

Old days of innocence and peace
  Came vividly to view,
And scenes of home, and love, and joy,
  His early childhood knew,
Ere greed of gain had drawn his soul
  From love of good and true.

The homestead, with its glad delight,
  The school-house on the hill,
The church whose spire rose high and white,
  The brook which turned the mill, —
As erst they lived within his sight,
  He saw them plainly still.

And early love's sweet garlands shone
  His dreamy thoughts among;
He heard the same familiar tone
  That young affection sung,
When buoyant hope his horizon
  With bright creations hung.

He marked the change — alas! the change —
  When, leaving all for gold,
He quenched the fires of early truth
  With lust's fell waters cold,
And innocence, a thing of trade,
  Was bargained for and sold.

Then conscience, with a wand of fire,
  Brought his life-deeds to view, —

Portrayed them to his blenching gaze
 In colors strong and true,
And fancies of appalling shape
 Across his vision flew :

The squalid forms of blasted ones,
 The hollow, sunken eyes,
Which beamed of old like radiant suns,
 And cheeks of healthful dyes,
Grown haggard now as hideous things
 That from the grave might rise.

And where the light of genius shone,
 And reason's blessed ray,
That light was quenched, that ray had gone,
 The curse now held its sway;
O woe! the peril of that one
 Who thus that soul could slay!

And maiden innocence and ruth,
 That once bloomed but to bless,
Whose smile was fraught with love and truth,
 Angelic scarcely less,
Sunk, sunk beneath the tempter's wiles,
 To utter wretchedness!

And dire distress on every side,
 And squalor, death and need,
And homes of happiness denied,
 And hearts that hourly bleed,

And little orphan hands upraised,
  In timid suppliance plead.

And sounds of woe rise on the air —
  Sounds that he heeds full well:
The mother's accents of despair,
  The reeling madman's yell,
The murdered victim's dying prayer,
  The murderer's funeral knell.

His eyes and ears drank in the whole,
  Chill grew his sluggish blood,
The while remorse poured o'er his soul
  An overwhelming flood,
His hands he wrung in dismal dole,
  And trembled as he stood.

Ah, sad the contrast which he drew
  Betwixt his now and then,
As memory recalled the view
  Of those bright days again;
A devil now he seemed, to blast
  And scourge his fellow-men.

And conscience whispered in his ear —
  "This work of thine regard;
In sin's broad field for many a year
  Thou 'st labored well and hard;
For all that thou hast rendered here
  Shall come a meet reward!"

And then he vowed a fearful vow,
  Wrung forth with many a groan,
That through his life for evil past
  He 'd struggle to atone;
He waked — the room was still and dark,
  And he was all alone.

THE SEEDY OLD GENTLEMAN.

Something similar, fully as comprehensible, but not quite as good as the "Ancient Mariner."

ACROSS my way, for many a day,
  I 've seen that old man pass;
He seemeth tough, and poor enough,
  And like to be, alas!

The poet seeth a seedy individual, and greatly commiserateth him.

I 'll seize my friend who here doth wend,
  To learn his story drear;
I 'll chain my friend, unto the end,
  Like the Ancient Marinere.

He would hear his story.

My friend draws nigh, I catch his eye,
  He falls within its spell; —
See yon man old, I would be told
  How he from fortune fell.

His friend falleth beneath the influence of a spell.

He hears me speak — pale grows his cheek,
  His lips are deadly white;
His brows are knit, his teeth are set,
  His eye is icy bright.

Its effect on him.

"The bank will close, my chance I 'll lose,
  My note they will protest;"
But still with my look, like fish with hook,
  I held him in unrest.

He dreads the protest of a note.

"'T is nearly two — what shall I do?
  My note they will protest!
On 'change my name will be a shame,
  A byword and a jest."

The note still uppermost.

But by my spell I bade him tell
  That old man's seedy fate;
"You shall not go till this I know,
  Though you were ten times late."

His tormentor inexorable.

Then spoke that man, while tremors ran
  Along his spell-bound frame, —
"His story well I 'd like to tell,
  His fortune and his name;

He speaketh, and what he did say.

"But this pray hear, nor be severe,
  Though I should thwart your plan,
I cannot tell his story well, —
  I do not know the man."

Does n't know anything about the old covey.

THE PRINTER'S SORROWS ENDED.

ON THE DEATH OF S. J. BELCHER, PRINTER.

WHEN the summer beamed in its beauty,
That season of joy and mirth,
The cold, cold hand of sickness
Was laid on a child of earth:
A nobler spirit ne'er blest a friend,
Or gladdened a household hearth.

The fair seasons waned and faded,
The dreary winter came,
And day by day saw pale away
His life's dull, glimmering flame;
Saw, too, expire the cherished hopes
Of friends in deed and name.

Faithfully they watched beside him;
His eye so brightly beamed
With the fire of old intelligence,
So hopefully it gleamed,
The approach of the dread Destroyer
Far off they fondly deemed.

But his step in the silent chamber
  Was soon too plainly known,
And the object of a thousand loves
  Was claimed as his alone;
The pulse was stilled, and the eye was closed
  Of late so bright that shone.

Then friends met round the unheeding clay,
  With sorrow, to bid adieu
To the loved one, to be laid away
  Forever from their view;
And many a heart beat wofully
  For the loss of a friend so true.

And many a tear from woman's eyes
  Fell warm for the early dead,
Who, far from his home, in a stranger land,
  Had bowed to doom his head;
They had ministered to him hopefully,
  Till every hope had fled;

Bending o'er him at midnight deep,
  And again in the day's broad light,
Tenderly, most tenderly, marking
  The approach of his mortal night,
And smoothing his path to its portals dark,
  As woman only might.

The cold snow crisped beneath our tread
  As we bore his form away,

In the dreary chambers of the grave
  To moulder to decay,
To be known no more, save in memory,
  Till the resurrection day.

And many a snow and rain shall beat
  O'er his unconscious dust,
But the eye of faith rises upward
  On the pinions of its trust,
And sees the enfranchised spirit
  In its home amid the just.

THE WITCH OF LYNN:

OR, A GOOD MANY YEARS AGO.

"Go not to-day on the broad, deep sea,
And trust not your shallow bark,
For well I know a storm there will be,
Ere another night grows dark;

"And the surges will dash your cold corse o'er,
And the shark-fish claim its own,
Or, mangled and stark, on a rugged shore
Will your ghastly form be thrown!

"The foul bird will peck out your jet-black eyes,
And the loud winds laugh through your hair;
Beware, beware how my words you despise,
Or how you my anger dare!"

O, the witch of Lynn is a fearful wife,
And well will she keep her word;
And he must bear a thrice-charmed life
Who has ever her anger stirred.

The young man launched his boat on the tide,
And dashed along through the spray,
The bright waves gleaming on every side,
In the glow of a summer day.

And light was the heart of that young man bold,
  As he sportively onward sped,
As free as the billows that round him rolled,
  Or the sunlight round his head.

But a cloud soon arose within the west,
  That curtained the windows of light;
A gloom came down on the ocean's breast,
  Like the gathering shades of night;

And the winds piped loud o'er the troubled seas,
  And frightened the ocean bird,
And the young man's bosom was ill at ease,
  For a well-known voice he heard:

"The surges will dash your cold corse o'er,
  And the shark-fish claim its own,
Or, mangled and stark, on a rugged shore
  Will your ghastly form be thrown."

Then a huge wave reared its hideous head,
  And rushed on him amain;
And his mind flew back, in the time of dread,
  To scenes he'd ne'er see again;

And a view of a misspent life was given,
  All marked and sullied by sin;
One prayer for mercy he raised to heaven,
  One curse for the witch of Lynn.

With quick resolve he seized an oar,
And smote the wave in its breast;
Enough — the tempest was speedily o'er,
And the billows sank to their rest.

Now rowed he briskly the billows o'er,
And cheerily neared the land,
And well-known forms on the sea-beat shore
He saw before him stand.

"Ah, well have ye come, for a wonder dread
Awaits you in yonder room;
For the witch of Lynn lieth cold and dead,
With a sudden and fearful doom."

And cold and stiff her body he found,
And, stranger than all the rest,
It bore no sign of bruise or wound,
Save an oar-blade mark on the breast!

A pious man said 't was the devil's seal,
But the young man said not a word,
And left the town — but, for woe or for weal,
No one in Lynn ever heard.

APPLES: AN ANALOGY.

"Buy any apples?" said a tiny boy,
  Whose bright blue eyes ten summers scarce had seen;
His youthful look had none of childhood's joy,
  And speculation triumphed in his mien;
A cunning glance accompanied the word,
  As if his eye the latent thought could trace;
Seeing the answer, ere his ear had heard,
  Written distinctly in the buyer's face.
"Buy any apples?" and, his traffic sped,
The boy and basket from my notice fled.

How like the child, thus practising his art,
  Is man throughout the busy act of life!
The mighty temple called the human heart
  With money-changing schemes is ever rife:
Apples the stock, of large or small renown,
  With low and lofty traffic is the game;
All practise it, from him who wears the crown
  Down to the lesser one of humbler fame.
"Buy any apples?" is the constant call,—
Some get "whole heaps," but more get none at all.

THE DEAD SAILOR.

An eve of beauty on a summer sea,—
  The waves were sinking gently to their rest,
And twittering sea-birds with a noisy glee
  Skimmed, with delighted wing, the ocean's breast.
The moon serenely from a cloudless sky,
  With heaven's own holy beauty in her ray,
Seemed, like a pitying angel from on high,
  To bless the dying sailor as he lay.

The strong was bowed; the mighty was subdued;
  Death beckoned with his shadowy hand away;
Prone lay the form which often had withstood
  Assailing horrors in their stern array.
Shipwreck and peril had essayed their power
  His death in darkest moments to achieve;
But harmless had he passed through terror's hour,
  To die, at last, upon that calm, bright eve.

Low rise his murmurs on the evening air,
  Murmurs of home and friends, far, far away;
A language strange he speaks,*—his thoughts are there,
  Where at this hour of eve his parents pray,

* He was by birth a Dane, though twenty years' residence in this country had so perfected him in our language that no one could ever have supposed him a foreigner, unless from being informed of

That this their son, the wanderer o'er the earth,
  May be preserved from perils and alarms,
To bring a contrite spirit to their hearth,
  And find forgiveness in their loving arms!

We saw him breathe his last, our messmate bold, —
  No word we spake, but gazed upon the dead;
Serene he lay, unheeding, stark and cold,
  And many a tear o'er that loved form was shed.
We buried him beneath the ocean waves, —
  A better sailor's tomb than earthly sod, —
The mortal of the man the billow laves,
  The soul, immortal, resteth with its God.

the fact. In his last moments (while unconscious) his language was entirely Danish, and we could distinguish but enough to convince us that he imagined himself amid the scenes of his youth, and was conversing with old friends.

RHYME ABOUT A BULLFROG,

IN A CITY APOTHECARY'S WINDOW.

Thine is no note to tickle gentle ears,
  Grim songster of the marsh!
  But dissonant and harsh —
Unlovely, as thy countenance appears.
Mournfully sit'st thou, gazing, day by day,
  With dolorous, dismal looks,
  Thinking, perchance, of brooks
In green remembered meadows far away;
Or on some cool retreat in distant bogs,
  Where the zephyr speeds,
  Whistling on reeds,
Chiming in harmony with thy kindred frogs.
I gaze upon thee, frog, and gaze in pity;
  A "rus. in urb." they call 't,
  I think, but if in fault,
In English thou 'rt a rustic in the city,
Like some old Israelite by Babel's stream,
  Solemnly sitting there,
  With sadness in thine air,
Spending thy days in one regretful dream.
Some call thee ugly, but they do thee wrong,
  And I for native beauty
  Will stand out as in duty;
Thou 'rt prettier far than many sons of song, —

Men of the hairy mouths, as if they 'd bite ye,
Roaring their crazy notes
From transatlantic throats,
Signors Bamboozleum and Lignumvitæ.
And we are fain thy sadness to beguile;
Rouse ye, my prince of frogs,
Throw sadness to the dogs,
And give us once the sunshine of a smile.
Alas ! he 's senseless as the nether stone.
He heeds not sympathy,
He sees, yet does not see,
He in the city's crowd is all alone.

FRANKLIN.

WRITTEN FOR A NEW YORK PRINTERS' FESTIVAL.

MOTHER of Arts! Thy children come
  Fraternal faith anew to plight,
As brethren round the hearth of home
  On some time-honored festal night;
To cast the harsh emotions by
  The turmoil of the world imparts,
And crowd the quick hours, as they fly,
  With melody from genial hearts.

All sorrows borne, or ills endured,
  Forgotten be in present joy;
Relax the nerve to toil inured
  In Friendship's beam, in Mirth's employ;
Most blest the season that can bring
  Respite from Care's corroding chain,
Where flowers of soul luxuriant spring,
  To make the saddened smile again.

Here, as we mingle souls to-night,
  One thought preëminent must press,
One topic to impart delight,
  That waning years make never less:

We speak the name that gilds our art,
  Impressed on Time's illumined page,
And cherished warm in every heart,
  The Printer's glorious heritage.

The name of FRANKLIN! And the blood
  Stirs quicker at its magic sound,
And busy memory brings a flood
  Of mighty deeds to ray it round.
And that great name, our cynosure,
  Will ever cheer us with its light, —
Like the north star 't will still endure,
  When our small suns have sunk in night.

Mother of Arts! We tribute bring
  Of honor to thy mighty son,
Whose praises every land doth sing
  That science sheds her light upon.
Our brother! 'T is no idle boast, —
  A proud affinity we claim;
And this to-night shall be our toast: —
  Our *brother-craftsman* Franklin's fame!

THE DISAPPOINTED FLOCK; OR, THE SHEPHERD IMPOUNDED.

A caution to peaceful people, with termagant wives, not to leave the key on the outside of the door ; and to flighty parsons, not to get so high that they can't jump down.

I 'M not inclined to swear the tale is true
  I here indite in affluence of rhyme;
Nor be precise in stating where or who,
  Or be particular in fixing time.

Enough for me there on a time befell,
  'T was said, an incident of teeming note,
Which gossips o'er their tea would love to tell;
  And mirthfulness did that same tale promote.

A Sunday in the melting, burning June
  Gave earth a sun that tried the people sore, —
The organ-pipes with sweating drowned the tune
  That struggled through their apertures to pour.

The church-bell, to its calling true, did toll, —
  Tolled till the tollman could n't keep awake;
And if its notes were bank-notes, every soul
  A most usurious toll that day did take.

The people gathered gravely in their pews,
  Gravely as was their wont on such a day;
Yet quite divergent were their various views,—
  The elders looked to heaven, youth t' other way.

And heard they still the bell's dull toll and toll,
  The neighbors wishing that its tongue were dumb;
And heard they still the dismal organ dole
  Its airs — the atmosphere of kingdom come.

And still the parson came not on the scene,
  Though long the hour had passed at which he ought;
Grave men looked round with a most meaning mien,
  And all were wide awake with wakened thought.

The deacon placed his forehead in his palm,
  As if the matter he would take in hand,
Then, rising with a Christian temper calm,
  He hemmed aloud, attention to command:

"I go, my friends," the good man spake, "to bring
  Some tidings sure of him we love so dear;
It surely cannot be a trivial thing
  To keep him from these courts, the case is clear."

Then wandered Deacon Jones from forth the church,
  And to the parsonage he went away,
Leaving the congregation in the lurch,
  To everything but prayerfulness a prey.

Imagination drew the hoof and tail
  And horns of demons with an aspect dire,
Who doubtless dared his reverence to assail
  For striving to throw water on their fire;

Or, taking to himself some siren's form,
  Old Smut had lured him from his calling high; —
They knew his heart susceptible and warm;
  They knew the tempter he would never fly.

And there they steamed upon that Sabbath day;
  Though temperate men, yet every man was hot,
Determined to the church to be a stay, —
  Like Lady Macbeth, could n't "out the spot;"

And where was he, the good man and the right,
  Who "waiting saints" were anxious should appear?
Alas! good Deacon Jones, he found him tight
  And fast within an upper chamber drear.

So upward did his heavenly fancy rise,
  His study graced his dwelling's topmost height;
Two pair of stairs would not his need suffice,
  His aspiration took another flight.

And there good Deacon Jones the parson found,
  Breathing the breezes through a skylight dim;
He heard the bell's toll echoing all around,
  But sad the story that it told to him.

A shrewish wife had turned on him the key,
  And left him there in solitude to pout;
Like Sterne's caged starling, prisoned close was he,
  Sighing, most dismally, "I can't get out."

* * * * * *

In order meet they all did homeward part,
  As they the tale of trouble soon did hear;
So sad the parson took the thing to heart,
  He left the parish ere another year.

I WOULD N'T—WOULD YOU?

I WOULD N'T give much for his spirit who 'd covet
And wish for his own a gem or a flower,
Who 'd silently long for and secretly love it,
And see it at last grace some other man's bower;
I would n't give much for such spirit, would you?

I would n't give much for the diffident lover
Who mopingly tenders his mistress his sighs,
And, whilst loving nothing that 's earthly above her,
Sees some more ardent lover run off with the prize;
I would n't give much for such lovers, would you?

I would n't give much for a parson who preaches
'Gainst vices and follies that life's path bestrew;
Who, maugre the moral his theory teaches,
In practice performs as all other men do;
I would n't give much for such parsons, would you?

I would n't give much for church-members who wrangle,
And sneer at whatever another may do,
With bitterness striving the fair fame to mangle
Of those who may wish other paths to pursue;
I would n't give much for such members, would you?

THE COAL-DEALER'S DREAM.*

O, WHY do you shiver and shake, Mr. Jones?
O, why do you shiver and shake?
  You tremble and sweat
  Like a poor man in debt,
  And your garment is wringing with wet, Mr. Jones,
  Your garment is wringing with wet.

Ah, me! what a dream I have had, Mrs. Jones;
Ah, me! what a dream I have had;
  I feel sore oppressed
  By a load at my breast;
  It is not *light weight*, you may rest, Mrs. Jones,
  It is not light weight, you may rest.

I thought I had *scaled* heaven's height, Mrs. Jones,
I thought I had scaled heaven's height,
  But was stopped by the guard,
  Who questioned me hard
  If I had credential or card, Mrs. Jones,
  If I had credential or card.

* Some years ago, during an angry altercation between the *Pathfinder* newspaper and the coal-dealers of Boston, the Dream grew out of the difficulty. Of course, it is only a dream.

I gave him my business card, Mrs. Jones,
I gave him my business card,
And when he read "*coal*,"
His voice seemed to roll
An ocean of dread o'er my soul, Mrs. Jones,
An ocean of dread o'er my soul.

I felt I was in the wrong *bin*, Mrs. Jones,
I felt I was in the wrong bin;
The guardian spoke,
And then, without joke,
My condition seemed blacker than coke, Mrs. Jones,
My condition seemed blacker than coke.

He spoke then my doom in my ear, Mrs. Jones,
He spoke then my doom in my ear:
"Leave, leave you this gate,
You are *wanting in weight;*
You are doomed to a darker estate, Mr. Jones,
You are doomed to a darker estate."

Then down I was hurled through the air, Mrs. Jones,
Then down I was hurled through the air,
And leagues on leagues passed,
Which brought me, at last,
To a cavern both gloomy and vast, Mrs. Jones,
To a cavern both gloomy and vast.

In vain I looked for a guide, Mrs. Jones,
In vain I looked for a guide;

Amid the dark air
I peered everywhere,
But there was n't a *Pathfinder* there, Mrs. Jones,
But there was n't a *Pathfinder* there.

And while thus beshrouded in gloom, Mrs. Jones,
And while thus beshrouded in gloom,
A door was oped wide,
And a scene I descried
I could n't describe if I tried, Mrs. Jones,
I could n't describe if I tried.

I *screened* my eyes with my hands, Mrs. Jones,
I screened my eyes with my hands
To shut out the rays
From a vast furnace blaze,
That burst on my night-wildered gaze, Mrs. Jones,
That burst on my night-wildered gaze.

The ruling passion was strong, Mrs. Jones,
The ruling passion was strong;
And though it was droll,
I forgot for my soul,
And thought of a contract for coal, Mrs. Jones,
And thought of a contract for coal.

As soon as they saw who I was, Mrs. Jones,
As soon as they saw who I was,
The door was shut to,
Without more ado,

And a voice roared the key-hole through, Mrs. Jones,
And a voice roared the key-hole through.

And these are the words that were said, Mrs. Jones,
And these are the words that were said:
"Crawl back to the dust!
You 're not fit to be curst,
Of all mean things you 're the worst, Mr. Jones,
Of all mean things you 're the worst!"

Then here I awaked by your side, Mrs. Jones,
Then here I awaked by your side;
'T is a frightful thing gone,
And I 'll try to atone,
And be fit for *some place* when I 'm done, Mrs. Jones,
And be fit for some place when I 'm done.

A SONG

FOR THE MERRY-MAKING ON WATER DAY.

Printed in the procession, by the Franklin Typographical Society, on the occasion of the introduction of Cochituate water into Boston, Oct. 25, 1848.

Away, away with care to-day!
  There 's naught but joy before us;
A gladsome shout from all goes out,
  And we will join the chorus.

All hearts are glad; each face is clad
  In smiles, delighted beaming;
There 's music rare on the autumn air,
  And banners gay are streaming.

The axe is still, the loom, the mill,
  The miser quits his treasure;
And every trade, 't would seem, had made
  A business out of pleasure.

And beauty bright sheds forth its light
  To glad the blest occasion,
And hearts to-day surrender may
  To coveted invasion.

This is no meed for gallant deed
  Achieved 'mid fields of slaughter;
Voice, bell and flame, with joy proclaim
  The Advent Day of Water!

Cochituate, inspired of late
  By generous ambition,
Left its still home to hither roam
  Upon a blessed mission:

It passed along with gladsome song;
  The meadows smiled to greet it;
And as each day it moved this way,
  Our spirits sprang to meet it.

Its journey passed, 't is here at last,
  And hailed with acclamation;
And every tongue shall swell the song;
  Whate'er its rank or station.

The thirsty mart feels through its heart
  The mighty current quiver,
Through streets and lanes, in iron veins,
  A subterranean river.

Unseen it comes to all our homes,
  To cheer the high and lowly;
Like gifts from heaven, unknown when given,
  But through their influence holy.

Exuberant force impels its course,
It rushes wildly onward;
Its fountain spray darts high away
In jets fantastic sunward.

Hail, hopeful stream! from thy bright gleam
Our hearts reflect the omen
That water's want no more will haunt
The thirsty man or woman.

Then let us join in nine times nine,
To greet the scene before us,
Till to the skies our shouts arise,
An universal chorus.

And ever may we bless the day
When Boston's sons and daughters
Came up elate to celebrate
The Advent of the Waters.

A TOUCHING BALLAD.

DESCRIPTIVE OF WOMAN'S FALSEHOOD AND TOO-CONFIDING MAN'S DESTRUCTION.

POOR Sam Brown dearly loved a maid—
  Fair Carabella Jones;
He loved her with his heart of hearts,
  And with his very bones.

And twice a week did Sammy go
  His Carabel to see;
Neat as a pin from top to toe,
  And light of heart, was he.

And Carabella often said,
  In tones quite far from sham,
There was n't anywhere a lad
  She loved so well as Sam.

'T was on a night of Saturday,
  And Sam was in a mart,
And bought his dear a true-love knot,
  To wear upon her heart.

"It is n't hardly ten," said he,
  And smiling shook his head,—
"I guess I 'll take it up to her,
  Afore she goes to bed."

Straightway he went unto her house,
And fancied her surprise
When this new tribute that he bore
Should sparkle in her eyes;

'T would add unto the brilliant glow
That brightened them before,
And make her heart, just like a well,
With joy to bubble o'er.

Softly he stept — said he, "I think
I 'll take her unawares;"
He opes the door, and — perfidy! —
How the poor fellow stares!

There, sitting by the kitchen fire,
Was a tall country chap,
With Carabella Jones, the fair,
A-sitting in his lap!

One arm of her'n his neck embraced,
Her cheek lay close to his'n,
While his arm her too willing waist
Most firmly did imprison.

Alas, poor Sam! he tore his hair.
Then left the house forever,
And threw his new-bought true-love knot
Far, far out in the river.

His heart was broke, he mourned to find
  Her false in whom he 'd trusted;
And soon he took to drinking deep,
  And soon he came out busted.

Oft passengers, the corners round,
  Would see him pensive standing,
His hat drawn down above his eyes,
  Each pocket with a hand in;

And, senseless as the very rock
  'Gainst which he was reclining,
All weathers were the same to him,
  If raining or if shining.

His form and face, once typical
  Of everything that 's jolly,
Seemed changed by elfin power to wear
  A marble melancholy.

And stiff they found him, one cold morn,
  Upright by that cold corner,
And people sighed to find poor Sam
  Had come to be a "goner."

And Crowner Smith this verdict gave
  On the unhappy fellow,
That he had found his early grave
  Through rum and Carabella!

YARN OF THE ANCIENT MARINER.

A BALLAD OF ISLINGTON CREEK.

Revealing certain fancied resemblances between a mill creek and other large ponds, with some reminiscences in point; but not much of a story, any how.

A TALL man stood upon a hill, —
  A mill-pond laved its base, —
The prospect wide that met his eye
  Was clothed in summer's grace;
"I'll ask yon ancient man," says he,
  "Some story of this place.

"It is a goodly scene to view, —
  I've travelled far and wide,
I've witnessed scenes in distant climes
  That shone in grander pride,
But for simple beauty, unadorned,
  This is worth all beside."

He bowed him to the old man's ear,
  Whom he saw sitting there;
The man was very, very old,
  And snow-white was his hair;

He seemed a patriarch, indeed,
Of venerable air.*

"My ancient friend," the young man said,
"What pond is this I see?
Its beautiful and glassy sheen
Seems fairy-like to me;
Is there no story for the scene,—
No unwrit history?"

The old man spoke,—"I 've grown gray old
On this, my native shore;
I 've seen far lands in my young days,—
I 've sailed the wide world o'er;
At last I 'm fast to moorings brought,
To leave my home no more.

"Bound to this spot, in miniature
I live anew my life;
I see again the surges roll
In elemental strife,
Or, gently rippling on the shore,
With pleasant music rife.

"And herein I can sail again
The voyages I have gone;
I brave once more old Boreas
Around the blustering Horn,

*The venerable man is now departed, leaving but a beautiful memory of his worth behind, which is fondly cherished by his son.

Or feel the burning eye of Sol
  In fiery Capricorn.

"When the sweet breath of summer draws
  From out the cooling west,
I revel in the genial trades
  That fanned my youthful breast,
When we flew along with stu'nsails set,
  By fear all unoppressed.

"And when the furious Equinox
  Lasheth the 'sounding shore,'
Dashing the spray with angry might
  The very house-tops o'er,
I hear again the heaving main,
  And tremble at its roar.

"And shipwreck's voice oft rides the blast,—
  A voice well known to me;
I 've seen fair proas bow their mast
  To the fierce gale's mastery,
And many a daring crew outcast
  Upon this mimic sea.

"And scenes of dread have met my view,—
  They 'll haunt me till I die;—
'T was yonder, in the rippling blue,
  That so delights the eye,
Where gentle waves make music true,
  Rose childhood's drowning cry!

"Here are my bays and islands too,
My gulfs, my channels, straits;
My grandson runs a packet-boat
To yonder mill with freights,
Unlearned as yet to speculate
In fluctuating rates."

"Where are the fruits, remembrancers
Of those you 've early seen ?
Where is the tropic's lavish yield,
Plantains and okroes green, —
The yam and tanyah, esculents,
You see not these, I ween ?"

"But we have better far than those, —
Talk not of roots like yams,
When we can dig, this beach along,
Such *groundnuts* as our clams,
The fat ones that we gather in,
'Twixt yonder point and Ham's.*

"Where is the orange can begin
With that gold pippin there,
To show such fair external worth,
Or with its taste compare ?
See where between the leaves of green
It glistens in the air."

* Ham's Point will be readily remembered by all Portsmouth boys.

"Shipwreck you state, and violence,
  But battle's brazen throat
Has never echoed round these shores
  Its wild, discordant note;
You could not have a naval fight
  In yonder timid boat!"

"Yes, but we had," the veteran spoke;
  "Yonder lies *Christian* Shore;*
It merited no peaceful name
  In distant days of yore,
For hostile hordes from thenceward came,
  Annoying us full sore;

"Until, in action close and warm,
  We drove them back amain;
We showered missiles on their heads
  Thick as autumnal rain;
They left us to our quiet then,
  And came not back again.

"But when the winter throws its arms
  Over creation wide,
And icy fingers gather in
  The circulating tide,
Come peaceful spearmen here with spears
  And axes panoplied.

* A part of Portsmouth named Christian Shore, though from no particular Christian characteristic that the writer could ever discover.

"And this, their winter calling, then,
  Similitude reveals
Between the one who dares new worlds
  To seek for fur-clad seals,
Or whaleman braving death for gain,
  And him who spears for eels.

"But now farewell; the waning day
  'Minds me 't is time for tea;
Go out into the world, young man,
  And think no more on me
Than if I were, like Ringbolt, sunk
  'A thousand miles at sea.'"

MY LITTLE ANGEL BOYS.

I MAY not see their features,
  Save in memory's faithful glass,
But I feel that they are with me
  Each moment that doth pass.

I feel them in the promptings
  Of good which thrill my heart;
I hear them in the voices
  Which pleasure most impart.

When the sun beams bright around me,
  And my soul is full of joys,
I then discern the presence
  Of my two angel boys.

They whisper solace to me,
  When sorrow's cloud is dark;
They fan hope's fading embers,
  When dwindled to a spark.

Their voice is sweetest music,
  But it greeteth not the ear;
The heart alone receives it, —
  The heart alone can hear.

As I lay me down to slumber,
Peace in my breast doth reign,
For I know my angel watchers
Amid the gloom remain.

Spirit eyes gaze on me,
Eyes that know not night;
Spirit hands unite to bless me,
Hidden from my sight.

Hidden, but, O, happiness! —
Faith assurance brings! —
Living, loving, still they 're round me,
Borne on willing wings.

LOVE'S VICISSITUDES.

Being an account of trouble in love, and a sad overturn of fortune's ladder.

JUDY CATHARINE O'BRADY,
   Long time ago,
Was "eddicated" as a lady,
   As she could show.

Servants had she ever waiting,
   Long time ago,
With ready hearts a-palpitating
   Her will to know.

Fine domains were spread before her,
   Long time ago,
Fortune's skies were smiling o'er her,
   Ne'er knew she woe.

Propitious seasons, in their seeming,
   Long time ago,
Wove fairy tinges in her dreaming,
   Of gorgeous glow.

But love, the wily little de—mon,
Long time ago,
Bestrewed her rosy path with evil,
As we will show.

Her heart to Tam McShane was given,
Long time ago,
Who followed diggin' for a livin'
Turf-bogs and so.

Secret was their love conducted,
Long time ago;
Her father could not be instructed,
His wrath would flow!

Duds and money, in abundance,
Long time ago,
Plate and jewels in redundance,
He had to show.

And, wealthiest he upon the Carron,
Long time ago,
Had willed that Kate should wed a baron,
She glad or no.

Their secret soon did he discover,
Long time ago;
She left the country with her lover,
Her all below.

Poverty soon found, nor left them,
  Long time ago;
Privation of their health bereft them,
  Death crowned the woe.

He drank iced water, when all heated,
  Long time ago;
And shared the fate to all those meted
  Who will do so.

And she, ah! sad was her condition,
  Long time ago;
She, the polished and the rich 'un,
  Or lately so.

Sad her end to write or hark it,
  Long time ago,
She retailed peaches by the market,
  And apples also!

ANGEL VISITS.

MAN in Time's low valley standing,
Brief the view his eye commanding,
Never changing nor expanding,
 Dimly seen through misty haze;
Circling mountains, purple beaming,
Lured his soul to constant dreaming,—
Ever dreaming, ever scheming,—
 On and upward was his gaze.

Hope portrayed with sweet prevision
Through the haze a land elysian,
Where no sorrowing or division
 Marred the paradisial scene;
Where, amid the bliss abounding,
Angel harps were ever sounding
On the ambient air surrounding,
 'Mid the smiles of Peace serene.

Thus the spirit ever yearning,
Still towards the mountains turning,
With a warm devotion burning,
 Pierced at last the obscuring haze;

When, adown the heights eternal,
Bathed in heavenly light diurnal,
Angel bands in garb supernal
  Recompensed its watchful gaze.

Distant seen at first, but nearer
As its vision waxéd clearer,
And the earnest soul sincerer
  For a closer union prayed;
When, the righteous prayer availing,
Downward on light pinions sailing,
Angels, with a love ne'er failing,
  Their bright homes with mortals made.

Joy is that fond union bringing;
Heavenly censers odors flinging,
Harps of gold with joy are ringing,
  Tuned to notes of bliss above;
Wreaths from bright celestial bowers,
Wrought in ever-living flowers,
Bind the care-marked brows of ours,
  Woven by angelic love.

And the heart no more shall sicken,
No more droop when sorrow-stricken;
Spirit ministerings shall quicken
  Hope and joy to brightest bloom;
And our voices join the chorus
Of the seraphs round and o'er us,
Hopeful for the race before us,—
  Fostering neither doubt nor gloom.

Still in Time's low valley standing,
Faith now views a scene commanding,
Radiant glories e'er expanding, —
  Mist no more the landscape hides!
And still comes a blessed legion
From that fair celestial region,
Who, with tender, sweet adhesion,
  In the homes of men abide.

THE MYSTERY SOLVED;

Or a caution to people not to think themselves better-looking than they really are.

I MET a friend in State-street, and he gave a leer and
wink,
I thought the fellow must be mad or silly made by drink,
He plied his thumb unto his nose, and laughing passed
along,
Amid the crowd of eager men that thereabout do throng.

And next a lady fair I met, and touched to her my hat;
She merely smiled a "how do ye," and shocking cold at
that;
And a pretty girl with laughter shook, who walkéd by
her side,
But why they looked and acted thus I knew not, if I died.

And queerly looked all men at me, — the stranger and the
friend, —
And nods and winks mysterious received I without end;
Each store I visited the clerks did whisper and did smile,
And the smooth-faced pampered villains did watch *me* all
the while.

The day was spent; I homeward turned, and sought my
dearest wife,—
Dearest, because the only one I ever had in life;—
The instant that she looked on me, she sank into a seat,
And with peals of laughter did she me her "lord and
master" greet.

Perplexed, I thought her crazy, and I stamped and tore
my hair,
The "mischief" seemed to haunt me here at home, and
everywhere;
I conjured her by olden love the mystery to explain;
She looked again into my face, and then she screamed
again.

She took my hand and led me up toward my mantel pier,*
And, with another burst of mirth, said, "Look in there,
my dear."
And there was writ the meaning plain of shrug and nod
and wink,
My face was smeared confoundedly, all over it, with ink!

*"*Mantel pier*,"—a poetical term, signifying a seven by nine cracked looking-glass in a wooden clock.

A PICTURE FROM LIFE.

I KNOW a gentle, quiet maid,
  Most quiet are her ways;
There 's quiet reigns in every look,
  In all she does or says.

Her garments wear a quiet air,
  And neatly sit the while;
There 's quiet in her low sweet voice,
  There 's quiet in her smile.

There 's quiet in her modest step,
  That falls with quiet grace;
There 's quiet in the rose's blush
  That mantles o'er her face.

There 's quiet pleading in her look,
  From eyes of quiet blue;
Quietly calm as heaven's self,
  And seemingly as true.

The quiet maiden has a home
  Quiet as can be found,
Shut in from city's dusty strife,
  And shielded from its sound.

It is a quiet mansion old,
   A solemn pile and gray;
Within its little shady court
   Quiet prevails alway.

A quiet tree its branches waves
   Before her window's view,
And breezes play in quiet mood
   Its verdant foliage through.

Heaven bless the quiet maiden,
   And keep her aye from harm,
And may her quiet ne'er be broke
   By trouble or alarm!

THE RULING PASSION.

An editor lay in mortal strait, —
   In sooth was near to death, —
About to exchange his earthly state,
   He spoke with a troubled breath:
I do not fear the cold, cold grave,
   I do not dread its gloom, —
I 've been too long but a galley slave,
   To dread a lighter doom;
But one thought gives me a darksome dread,
   As wanes life's flickering taper, —
Who is there left, when I am dead,
   That can read the proof of the paper!

THE VETERAN.

A STORY TOUCHING MIGHTY FEATS OF ARMS, WOUNDS, A CANTEEN AND A BRICK.

"Father, what means the frightful scar
  That marks thy aged cheek?—
Is it the fruit of bitter war?
  Does it of strife bespeak?
Or is it mark by Nature made,
  In some eccentric freak?"

"That scar, my son, did mark me long
  Before you breathed the air;
Vigorous was I, and young and strong,
  When that was written there;
It tells of scenes and times of which
  I 'll tell you when and where.

"Our patriot sires had made a rule
  That every mother's son
Should fully 'quip and arm himself
  With powder and with gun,
And take the field on muster-days,
  Ere he was twenty-one;

"And every heart throbbed ardently
The mandate to perform;
We rushed into the strife of arms
With emulation warm,
And many a warlike breeze we raised,
And many a mimic storm.

"Behold upon the kitchen wall
That old and rusty gun!
Full many a time the same I've borne
Till setting of the sun;
On training-days, you may depend,
Your sire was always one.

"'T was on a proud October day,
The sun shone clear and bright;
The lines were marshalled in array, —
It was a pretty sight;
The Bozzleton Light Infantry
Were ranged upon the right.

"The snare-drums beat their loudest note,
The fifes did shrilly play,
And banners waved upon the breeze
Of that great training-day!
A sham-fight was to be at noon, —
All panted for the fray.

"And every eye flashed keenly bright
To meet the scene of pride;

The officers, in fixings fine,
   Along the line did ride ; —
Our canteens, I forgot to say,
   Were plenteously supplied.*

"And soon the order to begin
   Came thundering down the line!
The enemy had taken post
   Right opposite to mine;
The Bozzleton Light Infantry
   Then opened on 'em fine!

"An aged man, who, 'up a tree,'
   The conflict stern did view,
Vowed that it had not been surpassed
   By aught since Waterloo,
Where, you will recollect, were slain
   An everlasting slew!

"We blazed away like blazes, and
   Our muskets rattled thick;
The smoke and fire raged frightfully,
   Our pulses travelled quick;
Now '*charge!*' the word, and in a fall
   Your parent hit a brick!

"Insensibly inglorious
   Upon the ground I lay;
They raised me from the battle-field,
   And carted me away;

*"I ordered the men to fill their canteens."—*Gen. Taylor.*

I was n't 'tight,' for I had drank
  But ten times through the day.

"Nay, do not thumb thy nose, my son, —
  It is not well, forsooth;
The story that I tell to thee
  Is simple, honest truth;
To doubt the word of reverend age
  Is very wrong in youth.

"And that 's the story of the scar
  Which on my cheek you trace;
I 'd like to hear the villain speak
  To brand it with disgrace, —
I 'd wallop him who 'd dare to cast
  Aspersion to my face!"

LAY OF THE LAST WHITE HAT.

A FALLISH ODE.

Not much of a story, but merely supposing what the last of the white hats might say.

WE 'RE fading fast away, Leary,
  We vanish from the pave;
The doom has passed that we must fill
  A fleeting fashion's grave;
The winds of autumn chill, Leary,
  Destroy us flowers of spring,
And here I lie, — thrown careless by, —
  An unregarded thing,

Thus glory has its day, Leary;
  When summer suns were bright,
The reeking apex, comfort bent,
  Found in us cool delight;
Alas! while we enjoyed, Leary,
  The season's honors tall,
We little knew how fleetly flew
  The hours toward our *fall*.

When Fashion dropt her "black," Leary,
  In summer's burning realm,
We were installed in favor then, —
  The "white" then took the helm;
Well we the goddess served, Leary,
  And ruled our little day;
Now "blacks" again resume their reign,
  And we are "cast away."

But, though we vanish now, Leary,
  Time must reveal our might;
The summer's sun will strike a blow
  To reinstate the white;
And when the heated poll, Leary,
  In lurid beams shall melt,
Then shall our sway again have way,
  Our influence be *felt.*

THE MAIDEN OF THE FOUNTAIN.

I SAW her in the soda shop,
  The choicest sweets among,
But sweeter were the words that fell
  In music from her tongue.

Those words were few and quickly said,
  But uttered in a tone
That made me feel the queerest thrill
  In every nerve and bone.

A red, red rose was archly set
  Within a glossy curl,
And sparkling brilliants met around
  Her little throat of pearl;

And love-provoking were her lips,
  Of richest cherry dyes,—
They added poison to the barbs
  That darted from her eyes;

Those barbs around me keenly glanced,—
  Most truly sent, alas!—
And amorous light like lightning danced
  Around the soda glass.

And then I vowed she should be mine,—
I 'd win her from the town,
And somewhere on a railroad line
We 'd settle snugly down;

We 'd woodbines have about our door
Trained to an arch above,
And chickens, children, pigs, would thrive
In sunshine of our love.

But, as my castle here had reached
Its climax just and tall,
Her *husband* stepped upon the scene,
And overturned it all.

"The melancholy days have come,"
And I was struck in June,
But "my poor nerves" are hardly yet
Restored to perfect tune.

Years may elapse,—no miles or time
Can e'er my love estrange,
Although a wretched dime I got
From her in making change.

CHARITY AT HOME.

THE door-bell rings with a terrible clatter,
And, wondering what can be the matter,
I rush to the door, with my face all soap,
  Lathered and moist for the morning shave,
Widely in haste the portal I ope, —
  'T is a charity boy who alms doth crave.
I give him a dime and send him away,
  'T were better than standing in chilly air;
And what so soothing to conscience, say,
  As the grateful tone of the beggar-boy's prayer?

The door-bell rings, — is company here?
Step and see, my Margaret, dear.
  More charity, say?
  Who is it, pray?
  Why and how are they coming this way?
    A paper is thrust in my open hand,
    That I the matter may understand:
  How Peter Von Swivel,
  With a face like the d——,
  Has been beset all his life with evil;
  How the burning mountain,
    Hot and heavy,
  Poured on the plain
    Its molten lava;

How escape seemed vain, and, no clothes to his back,
He left all behind him, alas, and alack!
And when safe escaped from fire and wrack,
The idea crossed his mind, in a crack,
That for freedom's fair land he 'd make his track!
Then he tells me in German, Italian or Greek,
That a word of English he never could speak,
That to work he 's not able because he 's so weak,
That the red is hectic I see on his cheek,
That seven young Swivels he has here at hand,
Whom he will produce, at my command! —
I give him, — 't were best, without a doubt,
Or he 'll beat me, some night, if he catch me out.

The door-bell rings, — what is it now?
My patience is gone! — 'T is a woman, I vow!

"Charity, sir, in mercy," she cries;
  "Give me food that my child may live;
Here on my breast the dear one dies, —
  Give me some food, in mercy, give!

"'Give us this day our daily bread,'
  Kneeling, I asked of God in fear;
Then I wandered forth from my squalid shed,
  And heaven has turned my footsteps here.

"My husband's life was worn away,
  Toiling and adding to others' wealth,
For which but our living from day to day,
  With ruined peace and broken health.

"Sickness came on him; he felt its blight,
Sorrowing laid he his head to die,
For us was his prayer through day and night,
For us was his last and dying sigh.

"Now begging we rove, my babe and I,
And bless us, pray, in our heavy lot;
There is not a gift God passeth by,
There is no good remembered not."

I saw, that night, the boy's pale face
Smile on me with angelic grace;
I saw the poor woman kneeling there,
'T was for me she knelt, and for me her prayer;
And old Von Swivel
Bore a look more civil,
And did n't seem half as much like the d——.
Then I vowed to myself I must always believe
'T is a better thing to give than receive.

A STORY OF A SERENADE.

A PATHETIC AND MOVING LOVE DITTY.

Lovers, with suspended breath,
Read this tale of love and death,
And, if to serenade you 'd roam,
Know first if your love 's at home.

On a last-summer night,
When the moon shone bright,
And the weather hot
Drove the pulse like shot,
Fond lovers were walking,
Sighing and talking;
Cits toasting and fretting,
And fuming and sweating;
All vigils keeping,
In vain wooing sleeping.

It was June, sweet June,
And out 'neath the moon
A lover "hot-pressed,"
With his passion distressed,
Would fain wake an air
To the charms of his fair.

He sung by her lattice, —
Her room window, that is, —
And, melting away
With the heat and his lay,
This was the song
That floated along:

SONG OF THE NIGHT.

O, come to your window, dearest!
And list to the lay I sing;
My love for you is sincerest —
I love you like everything!
The moon all my ardor is waking,
As it wakes up the tides of the ocean;
O, tell me that I 'm not mistaken,
That your heart feels for me an emotion!

Now, dearest, your dad 's in the city,
Come down and open the door;
O, do give some token of pity,
Nor let me in anguish implore!
While here on the boards I 'm a sitting,
The dew falls fast on my head,
My jacket is getting a wetting,
And the hope in it 's e'en a'most fled.

Such love as mine you 've ne'er known, love,
I 've never half told it before;
My heart shall be all your own, love,
If you will just open the door.

I love not for jewels or plate, love,
  My passion divides not with pelf;
And credit me true when I state, love,
  No female I love like yourself.

Thus he sang to the night, —
At the window no light,
Nor nightcap white,
Gladdened his sight;
No voice to cheer him,
And no ear to hear him,
Or, rather, the ear
That he wanted to hear;
No bright eye shining
Cheered his repining,
Its gleam compensating
Amply for "waiting;"
No vision half certain
Stirred the snow-white curtain;
When weary, down-hearted,
He home again started;
But naught could he borrow
To add to his sorrow,
When face to face met he
The damsel so pretty,
Who, with music outpouring,
He 'd just been adoring,
Talking most mellow
With a dashing big fellow!

He murmured adieu,
As she passed from his view,
And went home to bed,
With a brick on his head.

Despair then seized him,
"Schnaps" never eased him.
There came one morning
To the crowner a warning,
That folks had just found
A man that was drowned.
Then this was the verdict the crowner made:
That his aqueous friend
Had come to his end
By gin and water and a serenade.

ORACULAR PEARLS GATHERED FROM THE LIPS OF MRS. PARTINGTON.*

FIND nine peas in a pod, put them over the door,
The one who next enters is yours evermore.
When the rats rattle and kick up a "touse,"
'T is ominous always of woe to the house.
When the dog howls and moans your window near by,
Be certain it tells you somebody will die.
Drop a knife on the floor, and eight times in nine
You'll find it forebodeth a stranger to dine.
When your nose itcheth, it foretells of danger,
Or the kissing a fool, or seeing a stranger.
When you see a spark shine on the candle bright,
You'll get a letter before the next night.
When your right cheek burneth, as if in a flame,
Depend on 't some one is free with your name.
If the corns twitch and twinge which your pedals deform,
About that time look out for a storm.
If a black cat frolic and sport with her tail,
You may set it down as a sign of a gale.
If you laugh on a Monday in sportive delight,
You will certainly cry before Saturday night.

* The above are warranted *always* to transpire as predicted, *sometimes*.

Tip over the salt, and the fat 's in the fire,
Foreboding all trouble, dissension and ire.
Twirl a whole apple-paring over your head,
'T will fall the initial of him you will wed.
Sit on a table, it 's always a sign
That to speedily marry your wishes incline.
When the sparks briskly scatter from dry beech-wood,
There 's some one somewhere who means you no good.

THE LOST ONE.

HAST thou a journey gone, my brother,
That the days pursue their round,
Bringing to our wakeful hearing
Never more thy voice's sound ?—
No more shall we see the beaming
Of thy heart-fraught radiant smile ;
Angelic, more than mortal seeming,
That our woes did all beguile ?

We miss thee when the evening shadows
Fall sombrely our home around ;
We miss thee when the autumn breezes
Rustle the leaves with whispering sound,
Like spirit-voices gently speaking
To our sad bosoms, torn and drear,
Words of peace to hearts nigh breaking,
Thou hast left in sorrow here.

We miss thee when, with joyful greeting,
Friendship draws the heart along ;
We miss thy spirit in the meeting,
We miss thee in the happy song.

Thy seat is vacant, — sad the token, —
  We ne'er shall see thy form again;
Friendship's ties have all been broken, —
  Sundered is life's golden chain!

The journey thou hast gone, my brother,
  Man may never re-pursue;
Seasons change on one another,
  Life can nevermore renew;
But, though from our home departed,
  Though we mourn that we 're bereft,
Still will cheer the saddened hearted
  The bright memory thou hast left.

Ever we that memory cherish,
  And in love's undying flame,
Though our hopes and joys may perish,
  Thou art living still the same —
Still, as, when on earth, around us
  Thy mild influence was cast,
And the ties that early bound us
  Live enduring to the last.

OVER THE WAY LYRICS.

The "sensitive one" tunes his lyre in praise of loveliness discerned over the way, and sings:

O, BRIGHT eyes are shining there,
 Over the way,
With sweet smiles combining there,
 Over the way,
And like one enchanted,
By fairy spell haunted,
I 'm gazing, half daunted,
 Over the way.

Unheeding I 'm gazing there,
 Over the way;
There 's beauty amazing there,
 Over the way!
I 'm pierced through and through
With eyes black or blue,
Or of some other hue,
 Over the way.

All day they are vexing me,
 Over the way,
Their charms are perplexing me,
 Over the way,

Till this heart of mine
Fain would bow at their shrine,
And *all* own divine,
Over the way.

The "sensitive one" hears the sounds of music over the way, and he rapturously utters himself:

O, sweet the note ringing there,
Over the way,
Blessed thoughts bringing there,
Over the way;
Sweet voices swelling
Glad tales are telling,
All gloom dispelling,
Over the way.

Music sweet sounding there,
Over the way,
Rapture abounding there,
Over the way;
O, cease not its trilling,
O, cease not distilling
That melody "killing,"
Over the way.

Sing thou that strain again,
Over the way;
Let me not ask in vain,
Over the way;

'T is joy to my spirit,—
My heart leaps to hear it,
Fair minstrel, still cheer it,
Over the way!

A bouquet in the window over the way attracts the "sensitive one's" attention, and he compares:

That charming bouquet there,
Over the way,
Glows bright as the day, there,
Over the way;
But bright as its hues,
Wet in Heaven's own dews,
To compare, it must lose
Over the way.

For the blush of the roses there,
Over the way,
Less beauties discloses, there,
Over the way,
Than the red of those lips,
Which all flowers eclipse
That the bee ever sips,
Over the way.

The lilies can't shine there,
Over the way,
'Gainst charms so divine, there,
Over the way,

That neck, snowy white,
So dazzles my sight,
I' m half killed, or quite,
Here, over the way.

He misses a favorite face from the window over the way, and expends himself in an enthusiastic ode

TO THE ABSENT ONE.

I look for thee, dear one, in vain,
Thy fairy form I cannot see;
O, that my eyes might rest again
On what was late so dear to me!

Full oft I 've stood when morning's sun
Effulgent beamed there o'er the way,
And gazed, like an enchanted one,
To see thy needle swiftly play.

And day by day I 've vainly sighed,
As on thy lap thy work did rest,
And with sheer envy could have cried,
To think those trousers were so blest.

And then, when *thy* glance met mine own,
How sweetly beamed thy answering smile! —
A kindlier smile hath never shone,
Or one more fraught with fun the while.

My heart took strength amid its gloom,
  Thy glance the sun that cheered its powers,
Reviving it to fresher bloom,
  Like spring's warm sunshine on the flowers.

The "*Absent* One!" that cannot be;
  For though by fate we 're forced to part,
Thou ne'er canst absent be to me,—
  Thou 'rt ever present in my heart!

THE COROMANDEL'S LAMENT.

The following, supposed to represent the feelings of a Coromandel chief in captivity, was written for music. The incident is mainly true.

In the Coromandel country I was born,
  Far away, far away ;
And happy was I at night and morn,
  In the Coromandel country, far away :
    Where the birds sang free
    In the banyan tree,
  In the Coromandel country, all the day.

Ah, fearful was the fight where my father was slain,
  Far away, far away ;
Where first I felt the captor's chain,
  In the Coromandel country, far away :
    Where the breeze blows free
    Over land and over sea,
In the Coromandel country, far away.

Then cruel men bore me the wide waters o'er,
  Far away, far away,
From kindred and home I may never see more,
  In the Coromandel country, far away:
    From the green palm tree
    That overshadowed me,
  In the Coromandel country, far away.

But tyrants never can bind our dreams,
  Far away, far away;
Again in my sleep the warm sun gleams,
  In the Coromandel country, far away;
    Again on the tree
    Sings the bird for me,
  In the Coromandel country, far away.

O, welcome the hour when friendly Death,
  Far away, far away,
Shall waft my spirit with his breath
  To the Coromandel country, far away;
    Ever there to rest,
    In freedom blest,
  In the Coromandel country, far away.

A PICTURE.

OUR Mistress P. had taken her tea,
And had cleared up nicely, as ought to be,
And then beside the white pine table
Had seated herself quite comfortable.
The plated lamp by her side burned bright,
And scattered abroad its cheerful light;
And Mrs. P. sat with her work in her lap,
Her specs high up on the roof of her cap,
With her eyes upturned to the opposite wall,
Where hung the profile of Corporal Paul.
The night had sedately settled down,
And quiet rested o'er all the town;
Not a gust of wind was heard to mutter
Above the chimney, or shake a shutter;
And the atmosphere around seemed teeming
With all the elements of dreaming.
And Mistress P. sat in her easy-chair,
With her eyes on Paul suspended there,
While her thoughts were wandering everywhere.
But her chin soon sank to a graceful rest,
'Mid the folds of the kerchief on her breast;
Forgot she the world, its cares and its woes,
In the grateful calm of a fireside doze,
And fell from her cap her specs in her lap,
As Mrs. P. dropped off in a nap!

A WISH OF FRIENDSHIP.

Red Beach, Me., upon St. Andrew's Bay, is most charmingly situated, commanding a view of that beautiful sheet of water for twenty miles. The following grew out of a night's entertainment beneath the roof of an early schoolmate of the writer:

FAIR Nature here convenes her joyous court,
 And reigns with sylvan splendor o'er the scene;
Her banners gayly in the trees disport,
 And bird and wave and foliage praise their queen.

'T were blissful here to spend life's little day,
 To live 'mid beauties that enchanting press,
Where charms salute the eyes where'er they stray,
 And everything conspires the heart to bless.

Below, far-reaching, gleams the watery path,
 Whose gentle story falls upon my ear;
And graceful is the theme the water hath,
 Which my soothed spirit bows itself to hear.

My friend, thus happy in your blest estate,
 May no obtrusive care disturb the scene,
But Peace, fair spirit, ever on you wait,
 And crown your passing hours with joy serene!

'T is friendship's holiest prayer that Heaven may send
  A heart to feel the blessings round you cast,
That your own soul with Nature's charms may blend,
  And live in holy union to the last!

A PROPHECY FOR FIFTY-TWO;

THAT WAS NOT ALL VERIFIED, BUT WHICH SHOULD HAVE BEEN.

A "TO-DO" you have made about Kossuth, —
I admit he is worthy your praise,
But that I'm a greater than he
You will learn, perhaps, one of these days.
I 'll just put my carpet-bag down,
And show you the whole of it through;
There are rare things and mighty to see
In the budget of young Fifty-two.

They are not all fair-weather goods,
Are not all sugar and honey;
There 's much that is stormy and dark,
With a generous spice of the sunny.
Here 's a sword for the brave and the strong,
Its metal is tried and is true,
And use will be found for its steel
In the strivings of great Fifty-two.

Its gleam shall be seen from afar,
And Freedom's brave sons cheer its ray,
And sweep with the besom of war
Old Tyranny's strongholds away;

Then man shall stand up in his might,
With energy sturdy and true,
And vow e'er to cling to the right
Imparted by blest Fifty-two.

Here 's a promise of plenty and peace,
Rich gifts, I 'll scatter them free,
Strong ships shall stagger with wealth,
From every isle of the sea ;
Your garners I 'll crowd to the roof,
Your pathway with riches I 'll strew,
Till, blest to repletion, you 'll say
You are glad to have seen Fifty-two.

But here is a shadow of woe,
Like a pall most sombre and dark ;
There joy, on life's stormy wave,
Is a ruined and desolate bark :
Here the flowers that bloom by the way
Are nothing but cypress and rue ;
There many sad tokens will mark
The ravage of drear Fifty-two.

Here speaketh the voice of the storm,
And felt is the hurricane's breath ;
There Pestilence reareth its form,
And guideth the arrows of Death,
Here hearts are stilled — how still !
Which late such lovingness knew ;
There darkling fears, and sighs and tears,
Note the passage of Fifty-two.

Here 's a crisis for loving hearts,
  The kindling of Hymen's blaze,
And Cupid's arrows and darts,
  And flower-crowned wedding days.
And babies, and cradles, and such,
  Come merrily into view,
And infant voices make loud acclaim
  Of the joys of Fifty-two.

O, a budget most rare is mine,
  Brim-full of goods and ills,
From the destiny great of states
  To the settling of tradesman's bills;
And the plans of old Fifty-one
  I am bound to see "put through,"
For the seeds he sowed and guarded
  Shall blossom in Fifty-two.

But hark! my work must begin;
  I hear the old year's sigh,
As he turns himself in his bed,
  And makes a motion to die!
My mission I must perform,
  And my varied gifts must strew,
Now give a good-by to Fifty-one,
  And a welcome to Fifty-two.

CORA BELL.—A BALLAD.

WRITTEN FOR MUSIC.

Ah, Cora Bell! Fair Cora Bell!
  A brighter never smiled than Cora;
I loved her as no tongue could tell—
  As none I'd ever loved before her;
Her cheek was like the flush of day,
  Her eye as blue as Heaven o'er her,
Her breath was sweet as flowers in May,
  Ah, radiant was my charming Cora!
    Sweet Cora Bell! Cora Bell!

Dear Cora Bell! Loved Cora Bell!
  My gentle, trusting, loving Cora!
Her influence on my pathway fell,
  Like blessed light,—the heart's aurora!
My life seemed cast amid the flowers,
  My lot to spread their bloom before her,
And, living on through halcyon hours,
  In happiness lived I and Cora!
    Dear Cora Bell! Cora Bell!

Sweet Cora Bell! Bright Cora Bell!
  The angels claimed from me my Cora,
To go above with them to dwell,
  From my fond heart which did adore her;
She drooped,—I saw my fair star wane,—
  In saddest grief did I deplore her,
And long 't will be ere I restrain
  The bitter tears I shed for Cora!
    Lost Cora Bell! Cora Bell!

Dear Cora Bell! Blest Cora Bell!
  My loved, my lost, my angel Cora;
Her voice now joins the rapturous swell
  Of angel-harps around and o'er her.
Yet when in grief—my heart all riven—
  I on my bended knees implore her,
The sweet hope to my soul is given,
  In bliss above I 'll meet my Cora!
    Blest Cora Bell! Cora Bell!

WINTER BLOSSOMS.

Of brilliant hue,
Sparkling with dew,
Spring-flowers blush in the sunlight glow;
Their rich array
Strews the path of May,
While the air is glad with perfumes they throw.

The summer is bright
With forms of delight,
And Heaven's own glory is pictured in earth;
The summer-flowers,
Like summer-showers,
Revive old joys and give new ones birth.

But when Winter drear
Is king of the year,
And sheds from his hand on tree and spray
His blossoms of white,
So pearly bright,
It is richer to me than the glory of May.

O white, all white,
Like a bride at night,
Are the blossoms of winter which deck the bough,
And they flash as gay,
In the sun's bright ray,
As the wreath which crowns the spring's young brow.

MEDICAL.

When Stuffle's health by luxury had flown,
Changed grew his cheek and changed his voice's tone;
He begged the doctor his disease to quell,
But yet by *gentle* means to make him well.
"Give up your feasting," Galen made reply.
The spirit fled from Stuffle's pleading eye;
"I' faith," said he, and thought upon his larder,
"I know no medicine that could be harder.
Bring on your jalaps, ipecac and squills,
Your salts and draughts, cantharides and pills;
I'll take 'em all, as I'm a living sinner,—
'T were easier far than giving up my dinner!"

A SIDE-WALK SCENE.

O, sturdy man! O, sturdy man!
  What tomb is this, I pray,
That openeth here its ponderous jaws
  Unto the light of day?
Hath Death annulled the little lease
  Of mortal man's estate?
Is it for manes of stricken ones
  That here and thus ye wait?
"O no, my darlin'; this, you see,
  An't no tomb, bless your soul!
But 't is a trap where people stows
  Away their wood and coal."

THE AUTHOR TO HIS READERS.

Kind friends, I'm always happy when you 're so;
It is my study, wheresoe'er I go,
To gladden, if I can, by act or thought,
The circle in whose limit I am brought.
I love a smile much better than a sigh;
I love to see a bright, mirth-beaming eye,
That speaks a heart where naught of gloom or care
Can present peace and cheerfulness impair;
I love to hear the music of a laugh
Better than dismal moanings, more than half;
And can I but one joyful thrill awake,
Feel that one smile has kindled for my sake,
Have kind eyes beam upon me in their mirth,—
A bright endorsement of my efforts' worth,—
Have warm hearts welcome me with kindly glow,
Without hypocrisy the veil below,
Have woman clasp my hand in warm embrace,
And childhood gladden as it sees my face,
The aged wiled a moment from their pain,
Smiling in dreams that they are young again;
Could I—but, ah! the fond delusions fly!
These may be left to worthier than I.
But should one smile a moment radiant flit
O'er the dull pages I have herein writ,
A pride I'd feel, to future care a bane,
And bless the thought that I'd not *tried* in vain.

SONNETS:

PUBLISHED AT VARIOUS TIMES, UNDER THE TITLE OF "WIDESWARTH SONNETS," — THE NAME, "WIDESWARTH," INDICATING THEIR SCOPE, EMBRACING THE EXTREMES OF GRAVE AND GAY.

SONNETS.

I.

ON A PICTURE OF LILLIE.

A TRUTHFUL page is childhood's lovely face,
  Whereon sweet Innocence has record made,—
An outward semblance of the young heart's grace,
  Where truth, and love, and trust, are all portrayed!
O, blessed childhood! Like the wakening day,
  The auroral flush bespeaks thy rising sun,
And spreads a roseate tint about thy way,
  And Hope's gay blossoms open one by one.
Sweet Lillie! As I gaze upon thy brow,
  I feel my heart expanding into prayer,
That happiness may e'er maintain as now
  The truthful seeming it exhibits there;
May after-life no bitterness impart,
But lie, as now, like sunshine round thy heart!

II.

DOMESTIC.

It smiles! Around its dimpling mouth see play
The first glad token of a dawning love,
Like the bright glow of newly-wakening day,
Or some new glory breaking from above.
It smiles! O, rapture! and the mother's heart
Beats with quick pleasure its bright gleam to see,
Springing from dawning consciousness, whose part
In after years her crowning joy may be.
There 's not a bright creation under heaven,
There 's not a pure in heaven or in earth,
There 's not an ecstasy to mortals given,
There 's not a thing of most exalted worth,
Can, in the mother's plenitude of joy,
Excel that first smile of her darling boy!

III.

MUSIC.

I love to sit here in the Music Hall,
And hear the choruses of mighty song
Arise and swell, and pour themselves along,
In fancied tracery upon the wall;
And rapture clothes the melody with form, —
A lofty mountain of stupendous sound,

That bears deep thunder in its breast profound,
And gives them utterance with harmonious storm;
Raising its height far up the fretted arch,
A glittering circlet round its lofty head,
From whence effulgent rays below are shed,
To aid my vision in its upward march.
The chorus stops, — the mountain is a plain, —
The circlet naught but plain gas-lights again.

IV.

PHILOSOPHY.

Let 's take the world just as it jogs along,
Nor grumble at the ills which may assail,
But trim our ship to the impending gale,
And watch her well the breakers rude among;
Ne'er growl with envious spite at others' fun
When our horizon bears no gleam of joy,
Or when misfortune with a dark alloy
Causes our cup with sadness to o'er-run.
Rather " Old Uncle Ned's " example see,
Who, when rude Time his teeth away did take,
And he could no more grind the loved corn-cake,
With resignation " let the corn-cake be."
How can it help bad luck to growl and cry ?
Be patient, — for our turn may come by 'n' by.

V.

CHURCH MUSIC.

Ah, dearly do I love the organ's pealing,
With psalm-tune holy or with anthem grand,
The while I drum the measure with my hand,
And gaze devoutly at the frescoed ceiling,
Where modern Angelos have spent their skill,
And mimic niche and pillar make display,
And shadows fling themselves in every way,
In independence of the sun's high will.
I love to hear the voice and organ blending,
And pouring on the air a cloud of sound,
Until, as with a spell, my soul is bound,
And every faculty is heavenward tending.
Bang goes a cricket! — Squalls a child, sonorous,
And earth's harsh discord drowns the heavenly chorus.

VI.

TO SPRING.

O, beauteous Spring! I ope my window wide,
To breathe the sweetness of thy vernal air,
While quick the pulses in their channels glide,
The vestal favors of the spring to share;

I hear the lambs make music on the hills,
  I see the violets in the verdant fields,
I catch the perfume that the bland air fills
  From myriad blossoms that the season yields.
The shooting vine hangs trembling in the breeze,
  And buds luxuriant grace the teeming bough,
The robin sings his song amid the trees,
  And Nature pours her notes melodious now.
O, Spring! Thy beauty admiration moves,
But—but—but—Mary, bring my cloak and gloves!

VII.

THE SNOW.

Now white and beautiful creation lies,
  Nursing its struggling germs beneath the veil;
On rushing wings the fairy snow-flake flies,
  Urged by the breath of the on-hurrying gale.
Now jingling bells thrill wildly on the ear,
  As vying coursers dart along the way,
Now rise in chorus tones of blithest cheer,
  As beams the moon with calm, untroubled ray.
I bless the snow! How fair its glittering sheen,
  How pure and holy is its pearly light!
Clad in its robe, the earth looks like a queen
  In the chaste vesture of her bridal night.
'T is passing fair,—yet, hardly fair is that,—
An avalanche, confound it, crushes in my hat!

VIII.

IN STRANGE COMPANY.

'T was in a 'bus we met, Thanksgiving Day,
  And side by side we sat, and *we alone!*
  The driver did n't see us from his throne,
And everybody looked the other way.
But she was chaste as ice, and pure as snow,
  And I could vow, though I knew not her name,
  Reproach ne'er dared to meddle with her fame, —
I pride myself a virtuous dame to know.
She sweetly whispered me that she felt giddy,
  And, with a gentle motion most divine,
  She laid the whitest little hand on mine,
And sat up closer, just to keep her steady.
Such confidence as this you 'll rarely meet
In earth's unsocial round; — it was a treat!

IX.

HUNGARY.

Poor Hungary! Our hearts are full of her;
  Our sympathizing bosoms quick unlock, —
  We pay our money out for Kossuth stock, —
And all our warm emotions are astir!
Get up a concert, — swift the tickets go, —
  The proceeds are for Hungary oppressed,

The purse respondeth to the ardent breast,
And dollars for Hungarian dolors flow!
But, ah! conviction comes too late to save;
We, not the tickets, 't is, that have been sold,
And rolls upon our mind the comfort cold
That we 've been diddled by a hungry knave!
Alas! poor Hungary, still we 'd aid her cause,
However much we may condemn Herr Krausz.

X.

ON A RECENT MARRIAGE.

JENNY LIND'S.

In ancient Bible times, — we read the story
In Numbers, chapter 'leven, — there befell
Among the Jewish tribes a famine sorry,
And all the Hebrews threatened to rebel.
Then Heaven, aweary with their ceaseless cavil,
Raised up a wind, — most marvellous of gales, —
And strewed for miles, on the encircling gravel,
Myriads on myriads of plumpest quails.
The moral of the tale I 'll not pursue,
Because disastrous did the sequel prove, —
I merely wish to show the modern Jew*
Revealed to us in epicurean love;
The ancient Hebrew feasted on his quail,
The modern Jew secures a Nightingale.

* When Jenny Lind was married it was understood that Herr Otto was a Jew.

XI.

TRUST NOT APPEARANCES.

"O WHAT a goodly outside falsehood hath!"
A smile may hide a cankering heart below,
A sunken pit lie covered by the snow,
A serpent lurk in the most flowery path.
Let not appearances alone delight you,
A pretty woman oft may scold like fury,
A jack-o'-lantern to a pit allure ye,
A dog with kindly seeming yet may bite you.
I passed a church, and workmen busy were
Repairing and improving its old style;
I stood a moment, and I could but smile
To see a mighty pillar lying there,
Bearing the semblance of the hardest granite,
But proving pine when nearer I did scan it.

XII.

MOONSHINE.

ROLL on, bright moon! And if we bid or not,
It would, undoubtedly, as ever shine.
How sweetly on yon bank its beams recline,
A radiant glory hallowing the spot,

Revealing rock and shrub in mystic show;
The tall trees rising steeple-like, and high,
Their forms disclosed against the western sky,
And flowers, moonlight-tinted, 'mid the glow;
Revealing lovers, vowing by that moon
Eternal fealty, everlasting truth,
And hosts of pretty oaths impelled by youth,
Rapidly made, and broken full as soon;
Revealing, too, 'mid country autumn airs,
Young men and roguish maidens "hooking" pears.

XIII.

FRIENDSHIP.

Friendship! Time-honored and romantic name!
Who hath not loved it that hath chanced to sit
Where Forrest roared it to a gaping pit,
When Damon gave himself to feed its flame.
But Damons now-a-days who hap to live
Are men of quite a different sort of mould,
And buying oftener than "getting sold,"
Asking more always than they wish to give.
An all-exacting thing is Friendship now!
Favors men ask and liberties men take,
And things enacted are for Friendship's sake
That wildest Enmity would not allow.
It is no use the sentiment to fetter, —
The fewer friends one has by far the better.

XIV.

TONGUES.

THE tongue is small, yet of a mighty force!
The Apostle James a homily once writ,
Wherein this useful member he did hit,—
A married man he must have been, of course.
A shrewish woman, with a wicked tongue,
Will strive to set a neighborhood in blaze,
A venom dwelling in each word she says,
And poison scatter peaceful homes among.
A tattling man,—a man in form alone,—
Will prove a curse where'er he chance to light,
Casting o'er tranquil scenes a mildew blight,
And changing kindred hearts to hostile stone.
Of all the tongues that I have ever known,
That to an ox-cart was the stillest one.

XV.

WIDESWARTH ON HIS PLANTATION.

THESE are my grounds!—a monarch here I 'm standing!
'T is here for me the tiger-lilies bloom,
'T is here the lavender sheds its perfume,
'T is here the dahlia towers with form commanding.

My grape-vines, high o'erarching 'bove my head,
  Wave their full clusters in my longing eye,
  And promise purple ripeness by and by,
When a few moons their changes shall have sped.
O, 't is a triumph thus to tread the soil,
  And feel that none but me herein bears sway!
  I envy not the rich, who, day by day,
For dollars' silvery music delve and toil!
See, in yon tuft of balm a honey-bee, —
Its song is music, more than dollars' chink, to me.

XVI.

OPENING THE MUMMY.

Unveil, sweet priestess! waken as thou 'rt bidden,
  That "the subscribers" may behold thy beauties,
  And wonder at thy narrative, if true 't is,
As 't is declared to them by Mr. Gliddon.
What antique fancy in thy look reposes;
  Perhaps thou 'st walked with Abram, venerated,
  Or with young Joseph chatted, consecrated,
Or in that distant day ta'en tea with Moses.
Great Mummy! wonderingly we thee behold,
  But thy old flesh is hard as nether stone,
  And for a wife we 'd choose a softer one,
For such as thou would make one's blood run cold.
Surely, old lass, you 're safe from Time's aggression,
His ancient teeth on you can't make impression.

XVII.

LEVITY.

Just think, one moment, what a sight 't would be
To witness sober manhood mad at play,
Trundling a hoop along the public way,
Or pitching cents, and screaming in his glee!
Or on the frog-pond sailing tiny boats,
Or on the common flying airy kites,
Or waging mimic wars in snow-ball fights,
Yelling defiance with shrill treble notes.
What to imagine! Yet did ye ne'er hear
The big church organ, consecrate to psalm,
Whistling profaner tunes without a qualm,
That sound to holy ears confounded queer, —
Dashing off wildly with a diddle-diddle,
Just like some little inconsiderate fiddle?

XVIII.

HOPE.

Through young eyes look we out on life's highway, —
The sun doth gladden it, and cooling streams
Murmur like pleasant voices in our dreams,
And pleasure beckons on with aspect gay;

Bright joys peep out from every covert lying,
  To lure the unwary to remote retreats,
  Holding up promises of rarer sweets,
Which as pursued evade the grasp by flying!
Bright hues soon vanish and the sky grows dark,
  The path uncertain cheats the weary eye,
  Realities beset we may not fly,
And hope 's diminished to the merest spark,—
Melteth away, like Whipple's "views," and leaves
Joy's phantoms only, o'er which memory grieves.

XIX.

LOVE.

Lift up your hand, and tell the angry tide
  Thus far to go, nor dare to break its bound;
Fix ye a limit for the scope of pride,
  Or bind it, humbled, to the very ground;
Check young ambition in its fiery course,
  When the prized goal is just within its reach;
Silence the tempest, with its accent hoarse,
  And bellowing winds a mild submission teach;—
These ye may do, and everything beside,
  In human province, mother earth above,
Excepting *one* that rule has e'er defied,—
  The heart's own choosing in concerns of love!
The heart will have its way, whate'er betide it,
As he and you and I and thousands more have tried it.

XX.

FAME.

What 's Fame? I ask — is it to live in story,
  That after days may eulogize thy deed,
Blazing upon a scroll with faded glory,
  Bragging of grandeur long since gone to seed?
Is it to raise a church, or found a college,
  That, ages hence, when builders' works decay,
From deep in earth, long hid from human knowledge,
  Thy name once more turn up to light of day?
Is it to fix thy mark where centuries' surges
  Wage tireless wars on its undying line,
When from their rimy billows it emerges
  And sparkles with a brilliancy divine?
I climbed a hill for fame, the way *I* "come it,"
And writ my name in granite on its summit.

XXI.

A QUESTION ANSWERED.

Ha! a red banner from the Old South swinging!
  What means this flaming "meteor of war"?
  Have outward troubles or intestine jar
Good men, but zealous, been to conflict bringing?

Or is 't in memory of those olden days,
  When horses occupied the cushioned pew,
  And contemplatively their oats did chew,
Right on the spot where Deacon Snodgrass prays?
The *red* flag hoisted on these sacred walls!
  Banner piratical, why swing ye there,
  With scarlet levity, on holy air?
On Christian heads thy lurid shadow falls.
I have it, — Thompson sells some pews to-day,
And that 's his flag that flaunts above my way.

XXII.

FAITH.

If you have faith, so holy writings say,
  You may command the sturdy sycamine tree
  To leave its quarters for a voyage to sea,
And straightway will the obedient thing obey.
Just so it is when ill, like mountain summit,
  Shall rise before us in the road of life,
  Let us press on with faith, and brave the strife, —
With this we 'll rise above and overcome it.
Ne'er doubting, like the preaching fool of yore,
  Who told his wondering, simple-moulded flock
  That, had he faith, a neighboring mass of rock
The weakest one could hurl a rod from shore;
But, scanning it again, began to doubt it,
And muttered, "*Faith*, though, I don't know about it."

XXIII.

RIDING.

Why should the rich despise the poor? — ay, true,
Why should they, to be sure? And why should I,
While in my coach, look down on passers-by
With scornful arrogance, as some folks do?
I will not; Jehu shall have ample sway,
I 'll let him take up all who choose to ride;
My coach has room enough on every side,
And he shall fill it, please he, day by day.
Come in, my crippled friend, we 'll find you place;
And you, stout lady, slow with fat and age,
Here you the ills of gout or corns may 'suage;
Come in, sweet damsel with the blooming face;
Come in; what 's this? What, hold your hand for pay?
A "bus," i' faith! thus grandeur's dreams decay!

XXIV.

DEVOTION.

Devotion 's that where, reverently bending,
The full heart holily itself outpours,
Forgetting all, save that which it adores,
Spirit and scene in one sweet union blending;

Not to glance sideways with a truant eye,—
  While holy words with fluent promptness slip,
  With ready eloquence, from off the lip,—
Watching each form or thing that flitteth by.
I knew a deacon once, a holy man,
  Who highest sat at church among the saints,
  And freest judged by all of human taints,
Who 'gainst all follies laid perpetual ban,—
Forgetful quite of sermon, psalm and prayers,
Watching two younglings courting on the stairs.

XXV.

SUNDERED FRIENDSHIP.

'T is a sad lesson mortals have to learn,
  That hearts will change and turn to very stone,
  And where the blessed light of friendship shone
The fell and deadly fires of hate may burn.
O, blessed Friendship! genius of our youth,
  That, all unselfish, pledged itself in need,
  I think on thee, and my sad heart doth bleed
To find thee fallen from thy primal truth.
O, bitter is it to pass coldly by
  The friend of early boyhood's happy days,
  Whose heart has grown estranged in selfish ways,
With unsaluting tongue and heedless eye!
But yet one thought occurs the woe to cease:
Perpetual silence is perpetual peace.

XXVI.

PHILANTHROPY.

SWEET bird, there warbling on the waving bough,
  My finger doth upon the trigger rest,
  And soon must cease to beat that gentle breast
That is so affluent with music now;
I do detest to kill thee, — manhood shrinks
  That late could shoot a man in Mexico,
  And unrelenting cause his blood to flow, —
Tears dim his vision, and the weapon sinks.
And yet so plump thou art, my darling bird,
  So wickedly provoking me to shoot,
  That, maugre all my qualms, I think I 'll do 't,
And kill remorse that lately in me stirred.
I must, — but, hang the bird! he's flown away,
It was n't safe for him round here to stay.

XXVII.

LIPS.

I SAW a rose-bud 'twixt a maiden's lips, —
  Borrowing new beauties from its ruby throne,
  And adding them to graces of its own, —
A bud the like the wild bee oftenest sips.

The sweetness of her lips did seem to lend
  A better fragrance than the bud possessed,
  And, as it rested on its station blest,
'T was joy to see their mutual beauties blend.
O, lips and roses! Once upon a time, —
  A kissing party 't was, — I "forfeit" paid,
  And kissed a somewhat antiquated maid,
Whom Providence had spared to mourn her prime.
Her breath made serious that playful jest,
Exhaled o'er *gums* not "Araby's the blest."

XXVIII.

CHILDREN.

Heavens, the racket! keep those children quiet!
  The house is trembling all from sill to rafter
  Beneath the tumult of their noise and laughter,
While carrying on their small domestic riot.
"Better to have ten rogues than e'er a fool,"
  Some one has said, in philosophic way,
  And that 's precisely what I often say
To soothe me for their disregard of rule.
"Troublesome comforts" at the best are they, —
  But, death-stilled be the music of that tongue
  Whose note the loudest through the house hath rung,
And what a cloud has fallen on our day!
Traverse the world, we 'll find, where'er we roam,
Few spots more cheerless than a childless home.

XXIX.

CALIFORNIA.

Good gracious! how the mind gloats o'er the stories,
Glittering and clinking with their weight of gold,
And never tiring, though so often told,
The last recital giving added glories!
We read them in the *Mercantile* and other
Veritable prints, and must believe 'em,
And eyes and ears are open to receive 'em,
And every doubt that they are true we smother!
But pile the metal on some mount Pacific,
Till we can catch its shining even here,
My bark, for one, shall never thenceward steer,
The faithful promise howsoe'er prolific.
The stories may be true, as we are told,
But there a beefsteak 's worth its weight in gold.

XXX.

THE DANCE.

The lamps in yonder hall glow grandly bright,
And music 'liveneth the midnight air,
And white-robed forms, than seraphs' scarce less fair,
Whirl fast and graceful 'twixt me and the light.

There youth and beauty crowd upon my sight,
  As through my half-closed curtains forth I gaze,
  To watch the sportive thread the giddy maze,
And smile in sympathy with their delight.
Delicious hour ! — enchantment rules the night ;
  The outside world is herein all forgot, —
  Here is their world, and pleasure all its lot,
And images of ill have taken flight.
Took flight ? — ah, no, — they only wait outside,
To join them in the coach, as home they ride.

XXXI.

REVENGE.

Search the long catalogue of wicked things
  That appertain to man's degraded state,
  In vain you 'll search for one more fell than Hate,
Or one that darker trouble with it brings.
With thoughts of malice rankling in his breast,
  The hater walks abroad a thing accursed,
  Consuming with the passion he has nursed,
And prematurely banished from all rest.
His victim to a grave his hate may bring,
  Or ingenuity some scheme impart,
  Furthering the promptings of a fiendish heart,
With constant woes a brother's heart to wring.
God marks the hater, and with just decree
Metes his reward in earthly infamy.

XXXII.

CHILDISH LOVE IRRESPECTIVE.

'T IS beautiful to see the childish heart
 Turning with fervor and a grateful force
 Towards the one who was its being's source —
A stream that ne'er will from its course depart.
I recollect, on one hot summer day,
 On Boston Common, where the trees had made,
 In the still air, a cool, luxuriant shade,
I saw a drunkard lying by the way;
His head was pillowed on a small child's knee, —
 A gentle girl, who, with most touching care,
 Fanned his hot temples as he slumbered there
Beneath the shadow of that spreading tree.
'T was like same pleading angel 'mid our sin
Watching, with hope, the lost soul back to win.

XXXIII.

THE OLD MAN TO HIS WIFE.

THOU art not beautiful, as men would speak;
 There 's care upon thy brow, and in thy hair
 A silvery thread I see gleam here and there,
And health's bright hue has faded from thy cheek;

But, O, the soul that looks from thy dark eye,
  And rests on me with all its olden light,
  Undimmed by time, with fond affection bright,
With love long tried and true, which cannot die;
Thy smile yet beaming with old kindness fraught, —
  Beaming like sunshine from the heart within,
  Which care, nor toil, nor poverty, nor sin,
Can dim, or turn its trustfulness to naught, —
These, O, my Nannie, draw my heart to thee!
I own thy chain, nor wish that I were free.

XXXIV.

DANCING.

Dancing some call "the poetry of motion,"
  Where gay danseuses nightly toil and spin,
  And Prudery, blind, or, seeing, chides the sin, —
But dancing such as this suits not my notion.
We see sweet childhood on the festal floor,
  And twining arms link little heart to heart,
  Where, banished all severities of Art,
Celestial Innocence her light doth pour;
Or at a husking or a sleighing 'bout,
  When quantity of quality takes lead;
  Or in a festal hour, long time decreed,
Men dance the new year in, the old one out.
These I do like, and I have laughed while gazing
To see a pair of thick boots in the maze amazing.

XXXV.

A SUMMER NIGHT.

'Neath the mild beauty of a summer night,
I leave my chamber to enjoy the air, —
To feel its eddies circling in my hair,
And feel it kiss my brow in wild delight.
The starry gems bestud the concave high;
O, blessed stars! on you I fix my eye,
And long for your bright spheres to take my flight.
Beneath o'erlacing elms, shut out from sight,
I stray, my head reclined upon my breast, —
My thoughts away, away amid the blest!
The world forgot, in my abstraction, quite!
Hark! there 's a sound of earth, a note of bliss, —
Of most ecstatic smack it is, I wist, —
Borne to my ear from darkness, comes a lover's kiss!

XXXVI.

UTILITY.

Man may win glory in the deadly wars;
In books may write his never-dying name;
In deep philosophy may find a fame,
And see its record blazoned in the stars;

In commerce may excel, and, on the main,
  A thousand keels rush swift to do his will;
  May with warm eloquence make tumult still,
Or wake the stillness to a storm again;
May with sweet melody attune his lyre,
  Till the rapt listener bows, forgetting all
  Within the power of its enchanting thrall;
May station gain, and compass each desire, —
Attain the acme of earth's greatness, maybe;
But what of all? — say, can he tend a baby?

XXXVII.

BE JOLLY.

Be jolly! drop the "minor key" of sorrow,
  Nor 'plain of troubles that may never rise;
  Make happy every moment as it flies,
And to its portion leave the coming morrow.
Long, dismal faces, and a dismal mood,
  Across our pathway should they chance to run,
  As envious clouds do muffle up the sun,
Drown all our joy as with a sombre flood.
O, for the heart to smile at every fate,
  Laugh like the old Greek in the antique story,
  Or, like Mark Tapley, still 'mid trouble glory,
And feel within its shadows more elate!
Give me a man that relishes a laugh, —
I'd trust him sooner than a gloomy one by half.

XXXVIII.

THE CHURCH IN A ROW.

LET dogs and other "varmint" take delight
In tearing, growling, worrying and biting,—
But when good Christian people take to fighting,
The heathen round about them laugh outright.
Fancy a temple with God's spirit fled;
Brother meets brother on the Sabbath day,
And furious saints belligerent fists do sway,
Or, with the fixins, break each other's head.
Curses ascend the roof, the air is thick
With violence, and holy spite, and malice,
And wrath is measured in a brimming chalice,
And Decency stands back, and Faith turns sick;
The Devil triumphs where Love should prevail,
And wags delightedly his forkéd tail.

XXXIX.

SUNSET.

THE Sun is sinking in the radiant West,
And over woods, and fields, and glassy streams,
Are thrown the glories of his ruddy beams,
Which earth with richer loveliness invest;

* In Chelsea.

And softening influences mark the hour,—
  The cattle meekly take their march for home,
  And low responsive to the sounds which come
Proclaiming gentle Evening's sovereign power.
Down 'mid the trees the golden sunshine floats,
  And the sad fife-bird pours his sweetest lay,
  The robin sings his vespers on the spray,
And myriad insects trill their pensive notes.
The Sun sinks slowly to his watery bed,
And draws a cap of cloud about his weary head.

XL.

RESOLUTION.

"I FEARED they 'd catch me, and I ran away!"
  Said a small girl, with basket on her arm;
  And, as if fearful of some threatened harm,
She watched her mother's eye of angry gray.
The hag her child had with the basket sent
  Into a neighbor's turnip-garden near,
  To steal; her little heart did quake with fear,
And her bright eyes dropped tears, as on she went.
"I feared they 'd catch me!" "Fool!" was the reply.
  The old one from its peg her bonnet took,
  Then snatched the basket with a sullen look,
While quick resolve shone plainly in her eye:
"The wicked flee when none pursue, you elf,—
The *just* are bold as lions,—I will go myself!"

XLI.

HOPE DEFERRED.

I MARKED an organ-grinder in the street,
And how he watched each window, low and high,
With most inquiring and artistic eye,
To catch the wish to hear his music sweet,
Retailed, like cider, from the barrel dark
That from his neck depended by a string,
The hearing which abroad its rapture fling
Would kill all wish again to hear the lark!
And still he walked,—no call from low or high,—
Jeannot from his Jeannette no moment fled,
And all unburied lay Old Uncle Ned,
And poor Susannah did n't deign to cry!
Hope's pedestal that organ-man might grace,
With expectation written on his face.

XLII.

MODERN NEWSPAPER PORTRAITS.

ILLUSTRIOUS men, of high renown and worth!
The tongue your greatness may not dare abuse;
Ye stand as beacon-lights in our small earth,
To praise whom enmity itself must choose!

Members of mighty councils in the state,
  Magnates of wealth, preachers of note and fame,
Heroes who honors share for service great,
  Savans who 'mongst the stars have writ their name;
Maidens of note, and dames of high degree,—
  You all are shining on the printed page,
But vexed I feel, as ye I daily see,
  At the vile scandal of this limning age,
That mars the lovely, makes good men a scoff,
In the "damnation of their taking off."

XLIII.

COUNTRY VISITS.

Delightful is it, when the burning sun
  Pours down in fervid beams that rival torrid,
  Frying the reeking sweat from the hot forehead,
From city dust and city heat to run
Where the bland air may cool the fevered blood;
  Where kindred beckons us with open arms,
  And Nature, smiling with ten thousand charms,
Woos us from grove and meadow, flower and flood.
But tarry not until that time doth come,
  When stranger's china disappears the board,
  And old familiar crockery is restored,—
The wish implied that we should be at home,—
When too familiar are the household tunes,
And iron take the place of silver spoons.

XLIV.

THE OCEAN.

O Ocean! One poor relative of song
  Poureth his votive tribute on thy shrine!
  Stupendous water-works! Whose source divine
Needeth no "act" thy durance to prolong.
An 'umble spirit his who bows to thee
  And freely yields himself to thy stern rule, —
  Though not as straight as those he drew at school,
And just the merest particle too free.
It needed not the might thou here hast shown
  To bring *me* down, — a very worm at best! —
  Mine's no unyielding stomach to contest
Power so omnipotent as is thine own!
No pious Jew, himself from sin to free,
E'er gave heave-offering true as this I heave to thee.

XLV.

WHAT I WOULD.

My boy! I'd have thee ever true as now,
  The guilt of falsehood ne'er thy soul to mar,
  And honor's light, an ever-beaming star,
To shed its radiance on thy open brow.

I' d have thee brave, and ever for the right
  Be ready with thine aid to interpose,
  To shield the weak, beset around with foes,
And raise the fallen by thy virtuous might.
I' d ask not riches for thee here below,
  For Care's perplexity doth with them rest,
  And love of wealth drives from the human breast
Sweet virtues that the humble only know.
I' d have thee happy in the heart's rich store,
Which, blessing others, glads itself the more.

XLVI.

SUMMER.

My heart springs glad to greet thee, joyous June!
  The flowers glow brighter 'neath thy gentle tread,
  And on the genial air their perfume shed,
While bird, and bee, and brooklet, all in tune,
Pour a grand symphony of love for thee!
  The trees are vocal, and their wide arms swing
  At breath of Zephyrus, whose airy wing
Disportive flutters in the sunshine free.
O June! My spirit fain would soar away
  To woody nooks, shut in from garish light,
  Where it might sing, from early morn till night,
To thee, bright season, sweetest roundelay.
We greet thee, June, a truly welcome comer;
We own that Spring is some, but thou art Summer.

XLVII.

SUNRISE.

Uprising from the trees, the gleaming gold
Of sunrise bursts upon my eager eyes,
And, as its glories to my gaze unfold,
My soul is rapt with wonder and surprise!
The green trees glisten in the radiance bright,
The birds their matin songs delighted pour,
The distant hill-tops catch the enkindled light,
My heart's devotion strengthens with the hour.
O Nature! may my soul still find in thee
A satisfaction sweet as now I know,
When, from the bonds of pressing care set free,
My bosom burns with admiration's glow.
I feel, while gazing here on Nature's face,
With Mr. Squeers, that "Natur' is a case."

Great Hill, Exeter, August, 1852.

XLVIII.

PATIENCE.

Patience, rare virtue, let me sing thy praises.
When gouty pains the human frame are racking,
How wretched is his plight who thee is lacking!
With thee more kindly rest the encircling baizes.

Patience! — The good dame sinks who has it not!
  Her house in riot, — "children everywhere," —
  Their voices loud disturb the quiet air,
And rude feet trample every guarded spot.
Patience! 't is needed in life's every round,
  And they are happiest who have it most, —
  Better by far than wealth is this to boast, —
It spreadeth sunshine wheresoe'er 't is found;
Patience, — but, O! it brightest shines in life
Soothing the tempest of a scolding wife.

XLIX.

JENNY LIND.

And do we hear thee sing? Or is 't some vision
  With melody celestial round us ringing?
Or some enchanting tones from realms elysian
  That waiting zephyrs unto us are bringing,
  And all around us like a spell are flinging,
Blinding our reason with a mystic thrall,
  Until forgot are the swift moments winging,
And present bliss becomes the all and all?
  The soul, inspired, from the dull earth upspringing,
Dwells in a newer, holier atmosphere,
  Where tuneful censers are with music swinging
Their cloud of sweets to feed the ravished ear.
The dream is o'er, — the error is forgiven, —
In Jenny's notes are less of earth than heaven.

L.

THE WOODS.

Ye brave old pines! I court your cooling shade;
  The circling air amid your branches sweeps,
  And, checked by you, the day-star's fervor sleeps,
Or here his hot artillery is stayed;
I from my covert view him undismayed,
  And snap my fingers in his burning face,
  As he peeps in where arching trees enlace,
And ask myself the question, — "Who 's afraid?"
Ah, many times have I thus onward strayed,
  In meditation lost, or sportive bent,
  Where every moment such enjoyment lent,
All other scenes were dull by contrast made.
My lad! your fancy now a trick has played,
You 're lost, as sure as fate, by the erratic jade.

LI.

TO MY FRIEND PETER.

I say, you rattling, hair-brained, funny Peter,
  Well do you shake us with your many follies,
  Driving forth from us all our melancholies,
With jovial exorcisms in prose and metre, —

We love you heartily, you funny creatur' !
  How could we find our way along without you,
  With all your oddities so thick about you,
And rare fun beaming out from every featur' ?
None in the fields of humor are completer
  Than you, my ever-ready pungent Snooks, —
  Though more a puncheon in your rotund looks;
True wit ne'er scintillates from any neater.
Salt keeps our meat and metre all the sweeter;
Attic 's the salt, and you are all salt, Peter.

LII.

WEBSTER vs. WIDESWARTH.

A SHOUT goes up, from patriotic throats,
  For Webster, mightiest of Columbia's sons;
The nation's flag from every topmast floats,
  And war's harsh thunder bellows from the guns!
'T is meet ye honor with a grand applause
  The men who make their mark upon the times,
Whether they move the world by potent laws,
  Or make men better by the growth of rhymes.
The laurel wreath by each could well be worn,
  And I 'm content, for one, to bear my part, —
Content, too, that the meed be likewise borne
  By all who merit it, with all my heart.
But Webster takes the whole, nor leaves for me
One single leaf from the undying tree.

July, 1852.

LIII.

SHAKSPEARE ILLUSTRATED.

"To what base uses may we come at last!"
  Ah! Shakspeare, what a truth thou here hast said!
There 's many an one whose lot seemed hopeful cast
  That in gray ignominy bows his head.
The youth that "goes it with a perfect rush"
  And claims alliance with the "upper ten,"
May find his fortune, like an eggshell, crush,
  And make him mingle in with common men.
I 've seen a maiden with a haughty air,
  That contumacious scorn did ever speak,
Glad in the servants' hall a place to share,
  And wash the dishes for so much per week!
It daily grieves my very soul to see
A barber's wig profane the bust of Ellen Tree! *

* Near Temple-place, on Washington-street.

www.ingramcontent.com/pod-product-compliance
Lightning Source LLC
LaVergne TN
LVHW020212110826
845151LV00003B/683

* 9 7 8 1 4 2 5 5 3 4 6 5 3 *